Before the
Pen Runs
Dry

Before the Pen Runs Dry

A LITERARY BIOGRAPHY OF SAMUEL HAZO

Janine Molinaro

Franciscan University Press

Franciscan University Press
1235 University Boulevard
Steubenville, OH 43952
740-283-3771

Distributed by:
The Catholic University of America Press
c/o HFS
P.O. Box 50370
Baltimore, MD 21211
800-537-5487

Cataloging-in-Publication Data available
from the Library of Congress
ISBN 978-1-7366561-1-2

Design and composition by Kachergis Book Design.

Printed in the United States of America.

For my family—whose steadfast love and support make all things possible.

For Bill—whose love, friendship, and culinary brilliance nourish and sustain me, and whose quick wit keeps me laughing every day.

Hazo is, as a poet and as a man, both cosmopolite and local, rooted in antiquity and in the Middle East and also in the present and in the state of Pennsylvania. In our fractious age—in which the cosmopolite and the regionalist are often at odds, in which sustained tensions between those of Arab descent and those born in the U.S. continue, in which a chasm expands between the past and the present—Hazo's life and work are a bridge that allows for the unification of apparent opposites, for harmony among apparent dissonance.—**Ryan Wilson**

Throughout his life, Samuel Hazo has sought to keep the living and literary word alive as a place where we discover the truth and the texture of human experience, so that we may hear the plain voice and see the honest facts of our lives, the weight of memory and the flesh, as well as the agile beauty of the mind that flits from item to item, thought to thought, until it sees things whole.—**James Matthew Wilson**

Writing in what I would call the Realist and Christian Humanist traditions, Sam's profound respect for the dignity and moral agency of every individual person comes through in all of his work. He owns his own voice so absolutely at this point; it's beautiful on the page, it's beautiful to hear him read it—and he's one of the best readers in the game.—**Mike Aquilina**

Contents

Introduction

On April 12, 2018, Samuel Hazo received a rousing, standing ovation from the audience members who came to hear his final reading as poet-in-residence at La Roche University. Aptly titled "Sam Hazo: A Circle of Friends," the event celebrated Hazo's invaluable contributions to the La Roche University community over the course of his eighteen-month residency. Students who had the privilege of registering for one of his poetry seminars attended the event, as did faculty, staff, and community members who had delighted in his eight-week evening course in poetry appreciation. Pittsburgh residents who followed Hazo's career and enjoyed his work also trekked to the small university in the North Hills of Pittsburgh, where I have taught since 1994, to pay tribute to this man whose writing inspired and moved them.

Standing with the military bearing of his youth as a marine, Hazo's alert eyes, droll humor, and sonorous voice enthralled the audience for an hour and a half with stories from his life and more than twenty recitations of his poetry. Despite the fact that he was eighty-nine years old at the time, it was a timeless evening with Sam Hazo. As I listened, I was touched by the music of his words and was as mindful as everyone else in the audience that this was an evening to remember. Although I have known him for my entire adult life, there is always something new to learn about him.

I first met Sam Hazo at Duquesne University in 1981. As an English literature major, naturally I had heard the buzz about his poetry writing workshop: a great course, everyone said, but Hazo had very high standards; don't expect easy. He was, after all, the founder and director of the International Poetry Forum, a Pittsburgh-based organization with global reach that hosted famous poets and performers from all over the world. He had also published eleven books of his own poetry by the early 1980s, so the prospect of learning from this highly acclaimed poet who hobnobbed with the other poetry "elites" was both exciting and terrifying. It also bears mention here that Hazo was handsome and debonair; in his early fifties at the time, he didn't look a day past forty. In short, he was an extremely swoon-worthy professor to the Duquesne University co-eds who flocked to his classes.

During our first week of the poetry writing workshop, Professor Hazo gave us the schedule of poets who would be reading at the International Poetry Forum that season and encouraged us to attend. There was no entrance fee for students, he informed us, so my classmates and I eagerly donned our nicest outfits and made our way to the Carnegie Lecture Hall in Oakland. The first two poets on the forum's schedule that year were Richard Wilbur (October 7) and Stanley Kunitz (November 4)—both of whom had won the Pulitzer Prize in Poetry. I was hooked.

Although my poetry writing workshop with Professor Hazo ended in December 1981, I became a dedicated patron of the International Poetry Forum, making regular trips to Oakland to see and hear such legends as Gwendolyn Brooks, Billy Collins, Terrance Hayes, Seamus Heaney, Jane Kenyon, Galway Kinnel, Maxine Kumin, W. S. Merwin, Sharon Olds, Linda Pastan, William Stafford, and Derek Walcott, just to name a few. In 2009, when Adam Zagajewski gave the final recitation and the forum closed its doors after an outstanding forty-three-year run, a significant and meaningful part of Pittsburgh's cultural landscape was lost.

Subsequent to that 1981 poetry class, my intended career path changed; I no longer wished to become a lawyer. Instead, after becoming ignited by inspirational and brilliant professors such as Sam Hazo and Albert Labriola, I decided to earn advanced degrees and become an English professor. By the time I finished my master's degree in 1986, I had devoured every book of poetry that Sam Hazo had written as well as his first novel (*The Wanton Summer Air*, 1982) and a book of lyrical essays (*The Feast of Icarus*, 1984).

Fast forward twenty-two years to 2008. Sam Hazo had retired from his teaching position at Duquesne ten years previously and was dedicating his full attention to writing and giving recitations. When I moved back to Pittsburgh to teach at La Roche College (which has since become a university) after teaching for eight years in Cleveland, Ohio, and State College, Pennsylvania, I was close to finishing my PhD. Still an avid Hazo fan, I remained in contact with him and repeatedly found myself asking him if I could write a book about his life and work. Frankly, I was surprised that nobody had beaten me to it, considering his forty-three publications spanning the genres of poetry, fiction, drama, essays, criticism, and translation. I firmly believed the world needed to know more about the man behind the profusion of publications and recitations. In his classically unassuming way, Sam always thanked me for my interest, assured me that literary biographies tended toward the tedious, and quickly changed the subject. But I would not be deterred. In 2008, Sam graciously agreed to meet with me to discuss the idea. In a tragic turn of events, just weeks after we met to develop a possible strategy for the book—which would involve many hours of recorded interviews with Sam—his beloved wife, Mary Anne, fell ill. We put the book project on hold for the next eight years while Sam cared for Mary Anne as her condition steadily declined.

On July 7, 2016, Mary Anne died—and a huge part of Sam's raison d'être slipped away with her. They had been married for sixty-three years, and Sam absolutely adored her. Everyone who knew Sam wondered how he was going to go on without her.

But something extraordinary happened at the funeral home: Sam asked me if I was still interested in writing the biography. I said I was, and he suggested that we start right away. Two weeks after Mary Anne's funeral, Sam and I met to discuss the book.

Given that Sam still did not wish to be the subject of a standard, wearisome, scholarly biography, we developed a new format. Through the lens of carefully selected poems, I would tell the story of this fascinating man's life and career—connecting the dots by providing essential backstories and details. The framework made sense. Much of Sam's poetry is intimate and conversational, open and largely unadorned—as Richard Wilbur described it, "a spare, sparkling flow of good talk." Readers feel a personal closeness with Sam Hazo; even those who have never met him view him as a friend—someone they have come to know and like. In his poems, says James Matthew Wilson, we hear "the direct voice of a man speaking out of the fullness of his character, and it is an appealing character."

In order for our proposed plan to work, the poems would need to be shared in their entirety instead of being excerpted, as is standard practice with most literary biographies. In essence, the poems would be central, serving the purpose of guiding the book as opposed to merely adorning it. Contextual details and the backdrop for his works would be my purview. Drawing on the wealth of insights Sam shared in his journal and the in-person interviews we held over a two-year period, this book is an intimate portrayal of the man behind the memorable words we carry with us long after reading them. As a result, unless otherwise attributed, all quotations are derived from the extensive transcript of interviews over the two years of our collaboration.

Two days after our first meeting, I received a note from Sam reminding me that he preferred the book to be "more biographical than analytical." He explained his preference by stating, "There are too many analytical books about authors and not many that see life as a story—which is what life is."

Over the course of the next two years, Sam and I met at least once a week at his Upper St. Clair home. I recorded our conversations about his family history, his life as a child and a young man, his time in the marines, as a teacher and football coach at Shady Side Academy, and as an English professor at Duquesne University. We talked about the International Poetry Forum and the more than eight hundred poets and performers he brought to Pittsburgh as guest speakers, his wonderful life with Mary Anne, their travels together, their son Sam and his wife Dawn, and the grandchildren. We talked about politics, friendship, war, gun control, Hillary Clinton, Donald Trump, the Middle East, and countless other topics. And although we talked a great deal about poetry, our conversations extended far beyond the poems that provided the basis for the book.

By the spring of 2017, the project had grown much larger than Sam and I originally intended. At this time, I had hundreds of pages of typed transcripts of our conversations. He had also given me his personal journals, which I was poring over and transcribing for documentation. In addition, I spent long days researching the Samuel Hazo Archive, housed at the University of Notre Dame, and I interviewed scholars who had studied his work.

In the summer of 2018, as Sam turned ninety, I began to weave my notes into a nonstandard biography of this uniquely talented man. In essence, the book is a retrospective of pivotal periods and significant events in his life that shaped the person and writer he became, and the individuals who profoundly affected his life by giving it hope, beauty, and love. The story is infused with the poetry and prose he penned about the decisive experiences that influenced him and the remarkable individuals who added their meaning to his life's collage.

Family holds a position of towering importance to Sam Hazo, as we can easily accede when we reflect on the essential contributions that our relatives make to our lives. I therefore begin the story in chapter 1 with his ancestry in Lebanon and Jerusalem, tracing the immigration path of his grandparents and parents to Pittsburgh. Chapter 2 details the significance of his liberal arts education at the University of Notre Dame, where he established the foundation for his poetic philosophy—a philosophy that he continually developed throughout his life. Chapter 3 follows his service in the Marine Corps and ultimate transition to a different kind of life in academia. Chapters 4 and 5 tell the beautiful story of his courtship, marriage, parenthood, professorate, and establishment of the International Poetry Forum—all memories he cherishes deeply and summons in his poetry. The final two chapters offer some insights into the poetic themes and subjects that he gravitated toward throughout his life. These chapters explore his view of the writing process as a relationship between a poet and the poem, and examine his poetic techniques. Most importantly, however, the final two chapters are a cognizance of Sam's unique ability to be himself and clearly speak the truth over more than sixty years as a poet.

As the reader will clearly see, Sam Hazo's life can be read in his poems.

But the full text of the poems is necessary if the reader hopes to develop a deep appreciation for his life and work. The poems included in this book are therefore primary instead of ancillary. They are the glue that binds the chapters into a unified whole.

JM
January 2020

Remembering My Father Remembering

We still can shun what shames or shams
the day and keep as one our vigor in the bond
of blood where love is fierce but always fond.

"Postscript to Many Letters"

In his 2018 book *The World within the Word*, Samuel Hazo explains the brilliance of John Keats's artistry: "For Keats, intuition of any beauty of form was almost invariably rooted in an intense sensory experience. James Russell Lowell has accurately described Keats as 'one who could feel sorrow with his hands'" (91). As the story of Hazo's life and work unfolds in these pages, the reader will see in his poetry a similar connection of the physical and the ontological. Expressions of beauty, love, spirituality, intuition, and a host of other intangibles animate the page as palpable experience. Likewise, aspects of the physical world—people, events, possessions—manifest as mystical presences that transcend time and space.

This seamless blending of the material and metaphysical worlds is perhaps most gratifying in Hazo's family poems, wherein he celebrates and memorializes his loved ones in a deeply personal, touching way. Family history, genealogy, and geography; kinship, love, and togetherness all hold quintessential importance to Hazo. There's no place he'd rather be than with his family, and this devotion figures prominently in his poetry. Some of Hazo's earliest poems (1950s and '60s) are tributes to family members: "For My Grandfather," "To My Mother," "Postscript to Many Letters," "Progenitor," "The Year I Reached the Years of God," "For My Aunt Katherine after Midnight," and "The Fathering," just to name a few. More than sixty years and thirty books of poetry later, Hazo's style and poetic technique have certainly evolved, but the intensity with which he honors his family in conversation and on the lines of the page has not. Author and friend Mike Aquilina says, "Sam is constantly revisiting conversations with his brother, with his father, with his aunt, with his son. It's all about close relationships with Sam."

Samuel John Hazo was born on July 19, 1928, in Pittsburgh, Pennsylvania—the city that would be his lifelong home and that he would celebrate in poems, essays, fiction, and drama; the city where he would teach English and direct the International Poetry Forum; and most importantly, the city where he would start a family and enjoy sixty-three years of wedded bliss with the one and only love of his life, Mary Anne.

Although Pittsburgh has been Hazo's lifelong home, his story does not begin in Pittsburgh or even in America. It begins instead in Lebanon and Jerusalem, where his mother Latifa and father Salim were born. Hazo's paternal grandfather was Assyrian and brought his sons to Jerusalem from Mosul, but he did not immigrate to America as his sons later did. Hazo's only way of knowing his grandfather, therefore, was through his father's stories. One of Hazo's earliest poems, aptly titled "Progenitor," pays tribute to this hearty predecessor who lived to see 110 years:

Progenitor

A stern, mustachioed Assyrian
who stalked the animals that Adam named
and searched the desert where the chariots
and all the legions of Sennacherib
advanced their blazonry toward the sea,
my father's father hunted porcupines
a rifleshot from Nineveh and Eden.

I know him only from my father's tales,
this Aramaic sire who brought his sons
beyond the havoc of the scimitar
by mule from Mosul to Jerusalem
and somehow lived a century and ten
before he died and left his youngest son
this son to hymn his bones in Babylon.

The family of Hazo's mother Latifa was from a small village near the southern city of Sidon, on the Mediterranean. At the time, the powerful Ottoman Empire was actively conscripting young Christian men to serve in janissaries, which were small military units that the Turkish army used to guard their possessions. Having no interest in serving the empire and with the full support of his family, John Abdou, Latifa's father, immigrated to the United States via Marseilles—first to Maine and then to Pittsburgh. Like many of his friends who became peddlers in Pittsburgh, John Abdou settled into the city and started a textile shop that made mattress covers. Little by little, he brought from Lebanon his mother Aphia, his brothers Joseph and Elias, his sister Katherine, his wife Zarifa and their two children—son George and daughter Latifa—Sam's mother, affectionately nicknamed Lottie.

Hazo remembers his maternal grandfather as a kind and generous man who seemed partial to Lottie, perhaps because she sang and played the oud, a pear-shaped string instrument much like a lute. Father and daughter often played and sang together, creating lasting family memories. When Hazo was a child, his grandfather occasionally sat on his bed and prayed softly in Arabic when he thought young Sam was asleep. Years later, when Hazo was a freshman at Notre Dame, he wrote an essay that described his feelings about his maternal grandfather. He recalls, "It was the first time I realized how words could evoke memories and could actually re-create how one felt at the time. It was an important discovery for me as a writer" (Journal).

Through memory, Hazo's poems reveal a deep love and respect for family members, as we see in "For My Grandfather."

For My Grandfather

Someone should speak a word for you
who after all lived only long
enough to teach us children's songs
in Arabic remembered now

with times you strung your lute alone
and plucked it with an eagle's plume
while we sat quiet, small and calm
and heard you sing of Lebanon

until our days of roundelays
turned brief as breathing, and the vengeance
of cathedrals tolled to silence
all your love and all your minstrelsy.

Mother Lottie

In 1904, when they were both young girls, Hazo's mother Lottie and his aunt Katherine emigrated from Lebanon with the intention of joining the other members of their family—father, mother, brother, and two uncles—in Pittsburgh. When they arrived at

SAM HAZO'S MATERNAL GRANDPARENTS, JOHN AND ZARIFA ABDOU

Ellis Island, however, they were both suffering with eye infections contracted aboard the ship. As soon as the immigration official saw their eyes, he determined that they should be sent back to Lebanon. Spurred by the devastating news, Lottie's father wrote a letter beseeching President Theodore Roosevelt to intervene on their behalf. Amazingly enough, President Roosevelt complied with the request and ordered Lottie and Katherine to be placed in the custody of Lottie's father.

Lottie taught herself how to speak and write English upon her arrival here—despite her formal education ending with elementary school. Because she was clearly brighter than the other children at Epiphany Elementary School, Father O'Connell, the pastor of the Epiphany Church, asked her to teach the other immigrant children English, a request that she graciously accepted. A few years later, she secured a job as a nurse for a Greek physician. Her strong desire to communicate with the patients—most of whom spoke only Greek—inspired Lottie to teach herself conversational Greek in a matter of just a few months. As previously mentioned, Lottie also played the lute and sang beautifully in Arabic. Her voice was so exquisite, in fact, that a pianist named Maloof who played with the New York Philharmonic invited her to New York to record some songs in Arabic while he accompanied her on the piano.

In 1926, Lottie met the first of four generations of men named Sam Hazo. Born Salim Hazo to an Assyrian family in Jerusalem, he and his older brother arrived in Pittsburgh via Mexico City in 1911. He settled first in the Hill District and eventually moved to Bluff Street—and at some point, Salim Americanized his name to Sam—*not* Samuel.

Sam and Lottie fell in love and married in 1926 despite objections from Lottie's father, who had a different idea about whom she should marry. The nature of the objection was probably religious: Lottie's family were Maronite Catholics, whereas Sam was Orthodox Catholic. At a time when such differences in confession were significant and a father's approval was important, Lottie demonstrated courage in marrying the man she loved. They married at St. Paul's Cathedral in Oakland, where Lottie would be buried just nine years later.

During their brief marriage, Sam and Lottie lived with Lottie's mother, father, and aunt Katherine. They had two sons—Samuel and Robert—who lived with them on Murray Hill Avenue before the entire family moved to South Negley Avenue, and finally to Wilkins Avenue.

In 1934, Lottie's mother Zarifa died. Then, on August 8, 1935—only months after she was diagnosed with Bright's disease—Lottie died. Her children, Samuel and Robert, were only six and three years old, respectively. Samuel Hazo's actual memories of his mother occur as mere flashes of events, such as hiding Easter eggs one Easter morning and swimming in the lake during a family trip to Lake Placid in the Adirondack Mountains. His memories don't exist for him on a continuum. He does, however, vividly remember moments toward the end of his young mother's life when Katherine would take him and his younger brother Robert into their mother's room in their house on Wilkins Avenue; there they would say their prayers and kiss her good night.

Most of what Hazo knows about his mother he learned from Katherine, who raised Sam and Robert after Lottie died. Lottie and Katherine (or Kak, as the young brothers lovingly called her) were approximately the same age and more like sisters than aunt and niece. They immigrated from Lebanon together and were essentially inseparable.

Fortunately, Lottie was survived by a small diary, a few letters, and countless anecdotes told by Kak and Lottie's father. All of this, Hazo laments, "made me truly regret that I never really had the time to know her" (Journal). He honors his mother—a beautiful, intelligent, hospitable, and courageous woman—in the following poems.

SAM HAZO'S MOTHER, LATIFA (LOTTIE)

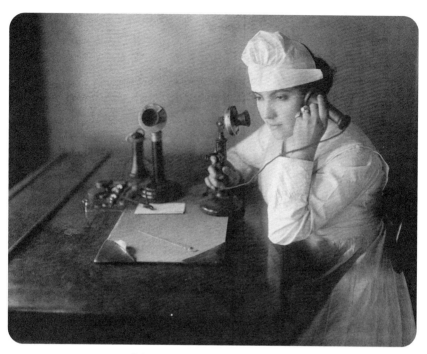

To My Mother

Had you survived that August afternoon
of Bright's Disease, you would be sixty-three,
and I would not be rummaging for words
to plot or rhyme what I would speak to you.

Tonight I found a diary you kept
in nineteen twenty-eight, and while I read
your script in English, Arabic, and Greek,
I grudged those perished years and nearly wept

and cursed whatever god I often curse
because I scarcely knew one single day with you
or heard you sing or call me by my name.
I know you were a teacher and a nurse

and sang at all the summer festivals.
You made one scratched recording of a song
I often play when no one else is home,
but that is all I have to keep you real.

The rest exists in fragile photographs,
a sudden memoir in my father's eyes
and all the anecdotes of thirty years
remembered like a portrait torn in half

and torn in half again until a word
deciphered in a diary rejoins
these tatters in my mind to form your face
as magically as music overheard

can summon and assemble everything
about a day we thought forever past.
For one recovered second you are near.
I almost hear you call to me and sing

before the world recoils and returns ...
I have no monument, my beautiful,
to offer you except these patterned lines.
They cannot sound the silentness that burns

and burns, although I try to say at last
there lives beyond this treachery of words
your life in me anew and in that peace
where nothing is to come and nothing past.

Hazo clearly remembers the old Lebanese folk songs his
mother sang in Arabic. In an effort to keep his mother's legacy

alive in the hearts and minds of his own family, Hazo shared the songs with his son Samuel Robert, a world-class musician, who in turn shared them with his daughter Anna, an aspiring young singer with a beautiful voice. The poem "Lottie" captures Hazo's memories of his mother and the impact she had on others.

Lottie

Her given name meant *gentle,*
　　but everyone called her Lottie
　　except the nuns.
　　　　　　　　They thought
　　Lottie was short for Charlotte.
As Charlotte, she taught, became
　　a nurse, and spoke with ease
　　in three languages.
　　　　　　　　As Lottie
　　she played the lute and sang
　　to her own accompaniment and once
　　with a pianist from the New York
　　Philharmonic.
　　　　　　　　After she chose
　　my father, he ordered from Damascus
　　a lute specifically sized
　　for her.
　　　　　　　　I still have it.
She cared enough to adopt
　　a Serbian girl until
　　her parents could immigrate.
In a one-line letter to my aunt,
　　she wrote, "Hi, sis, how's
　　your love life?"
　　　　　　　　She died
　　when I was six.

                              Decades back,
            a woman I'd never met
            stopped me and said, "I'm named
            after your mother."
                                        She smiled
                as if she'd kept a vow
                she'd made to tell me that.

Hazo displays the lute referenced in the poem on a shelf in his home office. It is inlaid with mother-of-pearl, and the face of it is ivory. He remembers the story Kak told about a lute handle breaking at the point where it meets the bulbous part. So she took it to a man who made guitars, and he told her that it was the most beautiful instrument he had ever seen. She asked if he could repair the lute, and he said he could. He kept it for several months before finally bringing it back to Kak. When she asked him how much she owed him, he said, "I'm not taking anything. It was a privilege to work on this instrument."

Father Salim

Hazo's father—the first Sam Hazo—was a man of excellent taste: in music, art, and especially in rugs. But that was not because of any benefit from formal education. Salim Hazo's family did not permit him to attend school as a child in Jerusalem. Instead, he worked in a shoe factory until he immigrated to the United States. Despite the disadvantage of illiteracy, he started a business as an oriental rug and linen merchant and made quite a good living. His wife Lottie taught him how to sign checks, and he memorized names of people and directions to cities up and down the East Coast. He traveled from Florida to the Adirondacks, selling to individual customers and sometimes displaying his merchandise at hotels. He knew real quality in merchandise and the value of

LOTTIE'S HAND-CRAFTED LUTE

money, and those important factors made him a successful businessman. He never tried to expand the business or convince his sons to join him. According to Hazo, "It was a one-man business; people knew and trusted my father, and that's the whole story." Nobody took over the business when he died in 1973.

In homage to his father's appreciation of the skill and beauty in the rugs he sold, Hazo wrote the following:

To Walk on Art

Hamadan, sirouk, bokhara—
such rugs can take a year
or more to weave.

                                    Colored
          with vegetable dyes, the hues
          intensify and blend the more
          the rugs are used.
                                    A royal
          bokhara requires three hundred
          hand-tied knots per square
          inch.
                          Conceding that only God
          is perfect, the weavers tie
          the first knot wrong by choice . . .
My father dealt in oriental
          rugs and knew each type
          by name.
                          He saw them all
          as more than goods.

                                    Sculptures
          and paintings were made to be seen,
          but rugs for him were usefully
          beautiful.
                          Often after decades
          he would buy back rugs
          from their original owners
          for the price paid or more.
He walked on oriental rugs
          with care as if in tribute
          to the weavers who went beyond
          art for art's sake to make
          what turned more beautiful with wear.

One of the most compelling stories that Hazo remembers about his father concerned a hitchhiker in New York. Conducting business just north of Rochester, Hazo's father received word that Lottie's health had taken a turn for the worse and she did not have much time left. It was nighttime and he was tired, but he immediately started heading home to Pittsburgh. He knew that he would have to drive through the night to get back in time to see her. Just outside of Rochester, he saw a man on the side of the road. Although he never picked up hitchhikers, something made him stop and pick up this man. As they were driving, the hitchhiker asked if something were bothering him. Hazo's father told him why he was driving through the night. The man observed that he looked tired and offered to drive while Hazo's father rested. He said that he knew Pittsburgh, and just needed to know what their destination was. Surprisingly, he told the hitchhiker where they were going and let him drive. His father fell asleep, and when he woke, they had just pulled up in front of the house. Hazo's father opened the car door without saying a word, ran into the house, and got to see Lottie right before she died. Afterward, he came out to thank the hitchhiker—but he was gone, and they never saw him again. Hazo insists that his father never was known to give the wheel to anybody—and he certainly never picked up hitchhikers. But he did that night, and it made all the difference.

Salim Hazo was a young man—only in his late thirties when his beloved wife Lottie died. After her death, he remained single for four or five years, focusing his efforts on working and taking care of his sons. The boys' grandfather and Aunt Katherine also helped, as they were all living together at the time. Their father then began a relationship with a divorced businesswoman named Lucy, whom he and Lottie had known for years. For some reason, Salim Hazo thought she was somewhat like Lottie. Even before they married, however, he learned that Lucy was not at all like

Lottie—and she apparently had plans to put the boys in military school.

Upon learning this, Aunt Katherine and the boys' grandfather sprang into action—suing to become their legal guardians. The case was heard in the Allegheny County Courthouse, and Hazo vividly remembers his conversation with the judge, who asked him where he would like to live.

"I would like to stay with my aunt and grandfather," Sam replied.

The judge inquired, "What do you do there?"

"I go to school and cub scouts," Sam replied.

"What will you do when you're no longer a cub scout?" the judge asked. And with the absolute conviction of a little boy, the young Hazo answered, "Well, you're always a cub scout!"

Aunt Katherine and Hazo's grandfather were awarded legal guardianship of Sam and Robert. Their father married Lucy, visited his sons on Sundays, and contributed financially to their upbringing. His marriage to Lucy lasted less than a year.

Years after divorcing Lucy, Salim Hazo married Yolanda Falvo. The boys liked Yolanda, and Aunt Katherine thought she was good for their father. Though the second "replacement wife" was better than the first, the family knew that she still didn't hold a candle to Lottie. Upon reflection, Hazo believes that his father was merely searching for a replica of Lottie, which his family never faulted him for. "I can imagine a man in his late thirties or early forties being suddenly left alone with two boys," Hazo explains. "I can see where he would have been lonely. I think a woman can cope with that kind of thing better than a man can." In the following poem, the language of silence and unspoken remorse reveals itself in the poignant final stanza.

Remembering My Father Remembering

He never recovered.
                            Passing
    the cemetery, he looked away.
Often he listened alone
    to recordings of classical poems
    of heartbreak sung in Arabic.
Lament as art both saddened
    and soothed him.

                           One night
in the Adirondacks, we drove
together to a mountain cove
and parked.
                    Surrounded by space
and stars, we sat, listened
and said nothing.
                    Later
I realized he must have come
there once with my mother
and wanted only to re-live
and share that memory with just
the two—the three—of us.

Aunt Katherine made sure that Sam and Robert remained close to their father despite living separately from him. Because Salim Hazo lived a good, long life, he experienced the joy of gaining a daughter-in-law (Mary Anne) and knowing his grandson, the third Sam Hazo. They all deeply loved Salim Hazo and took care of him when, at age eighty-two, he suffered a stroke. He remained very ill from the time of his stroke—around Memorial Day 1973—until his death on August 4 of that year.

Hazo's breviloquence perfectly captures the essence of his father's disposition at the end of his life.

The First Sam Hazo at the Last

A minor brush with medicine
in eighty years was all
he'd known.
                    But this was different.
His right arm limp and slung,
his right leg dead to feeling
and response, he let me spoon him
chicken-broth.

Later he said
without self-pity that he'd like
to die.
            I bluffed, "The doctors
think that therapy might help you
walk again."
                "They're liars,
all of them," he muttered.
                        Bedfast
was never how he hoped to go.
"In bed you think of everything,"
He whispered with a shrug, "you think
of all of your life."
                    I knew
he meant my mother.
                    Without her
he was never what he might have been,
and everyone who loved him knew it.
Nothing could take her place—
    not the cars he loved to drive,
    not the money he could earn at will,
    not the roads he knew by heart
    from Florida to Saranac, not the two
    replacement wives who never
    measured up.
                Fed now by family
or strangers, carried to the john,
shaved and changed by hired help,
this independent man turned silent
at the end.
            Only my wife
could reach him for his private needs.
What no one else could do
    for him, he let her do.

She talked to him and held
　　his hand, the left.
　　　　　　　She helped him
　　bless himself and prayed beside him
　　as my mother might have done.
"Darling" was his final word
　　For her.
　　　　　　Softly, in Arabic.

Kak

Aunt Katherine "deeply admired my mother," Hazo recalls. She
was not envious; she merely admired Lottie's "style, her intelligence, her ability to converse with anyone regardless of his or her
station in life, her gift of making people feel at home." Katherine's love for Lottie moved her to honor Lottie's deathbed request
that she take care of her sons—a promise that Katherine kept for
her entire life. Affectionately nicknamed Kak by Sam and Robert, Katherine remained single throughout her life despite being
courted by several men. Hazo believes she rejected the notion of
any potential husbands because of her responsibility to Robert
and him. She wanted to do right by them, to give them all of her
love and attention.

After Lottie died, Hazo and his brother continued to live with
their father, grandfather, and Aunt Kak. Once legal guardianship had been established but before Salim died, Sam, Robert,
and Aunt Kak all lived together in one bedroom in their aunt Anna's house on Shady Avenue—along with Aunt Anna's husband
Elias and their three children, Aphia, Gloria, and Elias Jr. Eventually, Kak and the boys moved to their own apartment on South
Aiken Avenue in Friendship, an East End neighborhood in Pittsburgh.

AUNT KATHERINE (KAK)

When Hazo was in high school at Central Catholic, a widower whom Katherine had known for many years asked her to go on a date. He arrived with flowers and great hopes of forging a relationship with her. But she rejected his advances, essentially acknowledging that they were both lonely, but pointing out that she had raised two young boys on her own and didn't need a man to help her. To Kak, being lonely was preferable to being tragic, which is what she believed she would have become if she had connected with a man for the wrong reasons.

Kak spent a great deal of time alone, a fact that Hazo thinks about frequently now that he's alone too. When Hazo went off to the University of Notre Dame, his younger brother Robert was still living at home with Aunt Kak. But after graduating from Notre Dame, Hazo returned home only briefly, opting in time to join the marines. Indelibly stamped in his memory is the image of Kak on the day he left for his service. They walked together to the streetcar stop—she on her way to work and he on his way to meet his group for Parris Island. Hazo's streetcar arrived first, so he found a seat and looked out the window. "There she was— just standing there and trying to smile—at a streetcar stop—all alone," Hazo recalls. He also vividly remembers thinking about the courage that took for her: "She had more courage than anyone I ever knew in my life."

When Robert left for St. John's College (and ultimately graduate studies at Princeton, the Sorbonne, and the American University of Beirut), Kak lived alone for seven years. Each morning, she would take two streetcars to Oswald Werner and Sons, where she worked as a seamstress. At the end of the day, she would do the same in reverse—frequently adding a stop at the store to buy groceries, which she carried three blocks to the apartment building and up three flights of stairs. She repeated that daily routine for seven years.

After Hazo's tour of duty with the marines ended, he came

SAM HAZO WITH AUNT KATHERINE AND BROTHER ROBERT

back to live with Kak, and they moved to an apartment on Harriet Street. Just two blocks from their South Aiken apartment, this one had fewer stairs for Kak to negotiate each day.

Kak was a remarkable woman in her dedication to her "sons," and when Mary Anne came into Hazo's life, she immediately understood Kak's importance. After their engagement, Mary Anne declared that Kak would not even be a topic for discussion: "She will live with us, period." And she did. She lived with them in their first marital home in East Liberty from 1955 until 1962, and she went with them when they bought the house on Somerville Road in Upper St. Clair that Hazo still inhabits. She lived happily with them until her death in 1964.

Kak's personality sparkled with a quick wit, just enough sass, and the courage to speak her mind in any situation. She also possessed a great sense of fashion and style, believing that a woman's poetry could be found in her way of getting dressed. Kak always said there was one thing she could do until she was nine years dead, and that was get dressed—in clothes of her choice according to her taste. Hazo shakes his head and smiles: "Although it was hard for me to accept at the time, in retrospect I see that it was so damn appropriate that Kak died one morning while she was getting dressed." Sadly, Kak did not live to see Hazo's son, Sam Robert, a fact that Hazo always lamented: "I would have loved for Sam to meet Kak," he said. "She would have taught him how to play poker!"

Kak

Her heroines were Pola Negri,
 Gloria Swanson, and Mae West—
one for glamour, one for style,
one for nerve.
     First on her scale
of praise came courage of the heart,
then brains, then something called
in Arabic "lightbloodedness."
        All
birds but owls she loved, all
that was green and growable,
including weeds, all operas
in Italian, the schmaltzier the better . . .

Lightning she feared, then age
    since people thought the old
    "unnecessary," then living on
    without us, then absolutely nothing.
Each time I'd say some girl
    had perfect legs, she'd tell me
    with a smile, "Marry
    her legs."
               Or if I'd find
    a project difficult, she'd say,
    "Your mother, Lottie, mastered
    Greek in seven months."
Or once when Maris bested Ruth's
    home runs by one, she said,
    "Compared to Ruth, who's Harris?"
Crying while she stitched my shirt,
    she said, "You don't know
    what to suffer is until
    someone you love is suffering
    to death, and what can you do?"
On principle, she told one bishop
    what she thought of him.
On personality, she called one
    global thinker temporarily
    insane.
              She dealt a serious
    hand of poker, voted
    her last vote for Kennedy,
    and wished us a son two years
    before he came.
                She hoped
    that she would never die
    in bed.
           And never she did.

"When you and your brother were young,"
    she said, "and I was working,
    then was I happy."
                        And she was.
The folderol of funerals disgusted
    her enough to say, "I'm
    telling no one when
    I die."
                        And she didn't.
One night she jotted down
    in longhand on a filing card,
    "I pray to God that I'll be
    with you always."
                        And she is.

Brother Robert

Born two and a half years after Sam, Robert George Hazo was not quite four years old when his mother Lottie died. Hazo says—although he has no way to prove it—that he always thought that Robert felt the absence of their mother the most. Young Sam certainly felt her absence like any child would, but Robert seemed to have the kind of temperament that their mother would have spoken to easily.

As they grew up, it became evident that Robert was extremely intelligent. Finishing Central Catholic High School with the highest grade point average in his class, he received a full scholarship to St. John's College in Annapolis, Maryland.

For Robert, the Great Books program at St. John's was everything that education ought to be: reading, talking, thinking, seminar-style Socratic learning. As an undergraduate, he studied political and economic thought and played on the college's championship badminton team. Upon graduating from St. John's—

ROBERT HAZO

again at the top of his class—he received a senior fellowship to Princeton, a Fulbright Scholarship to the Sorbonne, and a Rockefeller Fellowship to study Middle East politics at the American University of Beirut in Lebanon—with a side scholarship to the University of Baghdad. He became a well-known and highly respected authority on the Middle East, writing frequent commentary about it.

When Robert returned to the United States, he accepted a position at the Institute for Philosophical Research in San Francisco with famed philosopher, educator, and author Mortimer Adler. Before long, he was named associate director of the institute. Adler chose Robert to write the fourth book in the Concepts in Western Thought Series, produced by the institute. Robert's book—*The Idea of Love* (1967)—explores works of classical and modern psychology, theology, and philosophy that deal with all forms of interpersonal human love.

Robert's final career move before returning to Pittsburgh was to the headquarters of *Encyclopedia Britannica* in Chicago, where he was appointed senior editor for political, legal, social, and economic articles. In all, Robert Hazo spent twenty-two years living and working abroad and in states other than Pennsylvania. During his absence, Robert and Sam remained close, penning hundreds of letters to each other. Hazo wrote the following poem when Robert was living in San Francisco.

Postscript to Many Letters

While other brothers meet and talk like foes
or strangers or alumni—hostile, cool,
or banal—brotherhood is still our binding.
Somehow we have survived disintegration
since the quiet, Pittsburgh afternoons we walked
in rain bareheaded, scarfless, flaunting health,

the nights we smoked large, academic pipes
and read and talked philosophy, the years
of seminars and uniforms and trips
and letters postmarked Paris, Quantico,
Beirut, Jerusalem, and San Francisco.

Nothing has changed or failed, and still we have
"the same heroes and think the same men fools."
Our heroes still are individuals
resolved to face their private absolutes.
We see the fool in all who fail themselves
by choice and turn all promise cold with talk.
A Levantine who saw such folly done
two thousand years ago grew bored with life
and said only the unborn were worth blessing.
Not sticks, not any, not the sharpest stones
can bruise or break the unbegotten bones.

Yet, fools and our few heroes will persist.
We cannot bless the unborn flesh or wish
our times and cities back to countrysides
when wigwams coned into a twist of poles.
The future holds less answers than the past.
Salvation lies in choice, in attitude,
in faith that mocks glib gospelers who leave
the name of Jesus whitewashed on a cliff.
We still can shun what shames or shams
the day and keep as one our vigor in the bond
of blood where love is fierce but always fond.

Robert returned to Pittsburgh in 1970 to establish the American
Experience Program at the University of Pittsburgh. This program's objective was to offer important insights into political and
economic thought through lectures, discussions, and debates.

The program hosted many prestigious names in US arts and letters, including Shirley Temple Black, William F. Buckley Jr., Teresa Heinz, George H.W. Bush, Robert Novak, Geraldine Ferraro, Ralph Nader, Pat Buchanan, Dick Thornburgh, Sam Donaldson, John Kenneth Galbraith, Ted Turner, and Janet Reno. The program's success helped to launch it from its original position in the university's College of General Studies to the Graduate School of Public and International Affairs, and ultimately to the University Honors College.

Sam Hazo founded the International Poetry Forum in Pittsburgh in 1966, just a few years prior to Robert's return to Pittsburgh. Naturally, the brothers supported each other's intellectual pursuits over the years—Sam attending American Experience events and Robert attending International Poetry Forum readings. Maintaining a close friendship throughout their lives, Sam and Robert shared many beliefs and philosophies—including what it means to be genuinely educated.

Robert never married, although two women in particular energetically pursued him. When asked why he did not marry either of these women, Robert responded that he couldn't make the commitment—he just didn't have it in him. After an American Experience panel discussion at the Benedum Center on November 17, 2005, Robert announced his retirement. He died from heart failure on January 6, 2006—less than two months later.

Sam Hazo wrote "Morituri" for Robert years after his brother's death. *Morituri* is Latin for "We who are about to die," from the Latin phrase *Morituri te salutamus*—"We who are about to die salute you"—a phrase that, according to legend, was spoken by the gladiator to the emperor before combat.

Morituri

You don't know what you love until you've lost it.
—Federico Fellini

1

A man we loved is gone,
 a car he drove belongs
 to someone else, his house
 is up for sale, and we confront
 mortality each time we breathe.
Reduced to tears by memory,
 we learn the lost are always
 with us.
                And so they are
since love's the legacy of loss
and loss alone.
                        What's past
lives on to prove the legacy
will last.
                But where's the clemency
in that?
                Without the right
to bid or pass, we're picked
to play the merciless poker
of chance, and the cards, the cards
keep coming, joker by joker.

2

It's forty days to the day,
 and you're not here.
                                Last night
 I called your number by mistake
 and heard your still recorded
 message … "You have reached …"

It all came back—intensive
    care for days, one doctor
    who confirmed the truth, the nurses
    tending you as if you were
    their brother more than mine.
And all you asked was, "Sam,
    help me, for Christ's sake . . .
    I never wanted it to end
    like this."
                    And nothing else.
The day was the Epiphany, surnamed
    Little Christmas.
                    Monitors
    beside your bed recorded blood
    pressure, pulse, and every breath.
Before we left for lunch,
    we said our hesitant goodbyes.
You slept sedated, but the nurse
    assured us you could hear.
The last to speak was Sam,
    who carried both our names
    as dearest his mother insisted
    and whom you loved the most.
"Uncle Robert, we all love you,
    but now we're leaving for a bite
    to eat, and if you have
    to go while we're not here,
    it's okay . . . we'll understand."
He kissed your forehead twice,
    then held you in his arms.
Ten seconds later you were gone,
    as if his words had given you
    permission.

Later he told me
you parted your eyelids,
and your eyes were blue, not brown
as we had known them all your life.
No one could account for that.

3
Some say the three worst things
are losing a child, a mate
or a brother or sister.
                                Some say
the order's right, some say
it's wrong, but what's the point?
All losses to the losers stab alike
because they're all the worst.

4
You're buried in the same plot
with our uncle, our cousin, both
grandparents, our young mother,
and our great aunt who raised us
when our mother died and made us
what we were and are.
                                In the end
    it came to family after all.
By intuition or epiphany,
you picked your gravesite decades
in advance as if you somehow
knew what none of us
could know.
                        Just weeks before
you died, you said that death
no longer scared you though
you feared it all your life.

Later, we honored your bequests
    and sorted through your papers
    and effects.
                We learned you were
    the same in public as you were
    at home—but more so.
                      What else
    is there to say except,
    "So long for now, dear Bob."
Since brothers are forever brothers,
    you're here and elsewhere all the time
    for me exactly as you are
    and always were—but more so.

                For Robert George Hazo

TWO

And Learning Is King

We've journeyed back to grass and
   souvenirs and beige bricks.
The sky's exactly the same.
Acre by acre, the campus
   widens like a stage designed
   for a new play.

"Notre Dame du Lac"

For most of us, memories of college years are full of halcyon days spent debating and exploring ideas, heady nights of socializing, and the chance to forge friendships that would last the rest of our lives. To some, those years gave time to develop skills for postgraduate employment or advanced degrees. To others, like Sam Hazo, college offered the ability to delve into studies of literature, philosophy, and theology for the sheer enjoyment of it. Those years gave him time to see possibilities for the direction his life could take. The courses and professors at the University of Notre Dame were to significantly influence his future approach to literature, writing, and teaching. But when he graduated from Central Catholic High School, he lacked the financial means to pay for tuition, so he did not think he would be attending college at all.

As luck would have it, Hazo was in the right place at the right time: a high school graduation party for one of his Central Catholic classmates in the early summer of 1945. One of the guests at the party, a young woman named Myra Jane Barry, was aware that Hazo had been named Central Catholic's valedictorian, so she assumed that he would be attending a university in the fall. What she didn't know, however, was that despite his excellent academic record (3.7 GPA) and the honor of serving as class valedictorian, he had absolutely no prospects of going to college owing to financial constraints. When he told Myra that he would not be attending college because he had no scholarship and lacked the necessary financial resources, Myra told him about Leo O'Donnell, a Central Catholic alumnus. Dr. O'Donnell had attended the University of Notre Dame after Central Catholic and went on to become a successful physician at Pittsburgh's Mercy Hospital. He also happened to be a member of Notre Dame's Western Pennsylvania Alumni Association—an organization that awarded a four-year scholarship to Notre Dame to one deserving young man each year. (Women were not admitted to Notre Dame until 1972.) According to Myra, Dr. O'Donnell liked "to keep a boy from Central at Notre Dame" (Journal). Hazo contacted Dr. O'Donnell right away and was invited for an interview. The day after the interview, Hazo learned that he had edged out the competition and won the scholarship. He knew at that moment that the trajectory of his life had just changed, but Hazo would not realize until much later that his Notre Dame education would significantly influence the man he would ultimately become.

Less than two months after winning the scholarship, Hazo packed all of his belongings into one bag and boarded a train to South Bend, Indiana. Although he had never visited the campus, Hazo had seen pictures of Notre Dame in the Central Catholic yearbook. One picture he remembers vividly: the drum major for the Notre Dame marching band. His name, Hazo recalls, was Stan

Litazett—"and he looked terrific." At the South Bend train station, Hazo hailed a taxi and headed toward his new home. "You can imagine my awe as we neared the campus down Notre Dame Avenue, and I saw the dome for the first time." It was a moment Hazo remembers clearly because he noticed that "the gold on the dome was peeling off, and the economics of the war had prevented its being repaired" (Journal).

At Notre Dame, Hazo declared an English major with his sights ultimately set on law school. This was not, he clarifies, because he necessarily wanted to be a lawyer. Instead, he explains, he felt a certain family pressure to earn a degree that would lead to law school. Like most first-year students, Hazo had apprehensions about the difficulty of college-level academic requirements, but he soon came to appreciate anew the quality education he received at Central Catholic. "My courses in English and Biology were a snap, and four years of Latin [had] prepared me well for Spanish. I did very well in my freshman year, and my record stayed good for the rest of the time I was there" (Journal).

In his junior year at Notre Dame, Hazo started a two-year sequence of courses titled the Philosophy of Literature. The courses examined everything from Chaucer to Shakespeare, Donne, Thomas More, the Elizabethan poets—all of the consequential writers—through a philosophical and theological lens. This experience of intellectual enlightenment, Hazo asserts, shaped his entire attitude toward writing and literature: "The final judgments in literature are eventually theological and philosophical," Hazo explains. "There's no escaping that. If the vision of the author has no theological dimension . . . it's an incomplete vision of what men and women are."

The first year of the course was taught by Rufus Rauch, and the second year by Frank O'Malley. Rauch was a respected scholar, but unlike some of the more traditional members of the professorate, Rauch invited students to his home to discuss literature and theology in a more relaxed setting than the classroom. Hazo enjoyed these visits; he liked the *feel* of the home life of a professor, which, he says, "prompted my earliest inklings toward the profession" (Journal).

Those early inklings toward teaching were crystallized in Hazo's senior year at Notre Dame when Frank O'Malley taught the second part of the Philosophy of Literature sequence. O'Malley was a visionary who believed that a teacher should "lead students into the jungle and then let them find their own way out." Hazo remembers that O'Malley always challenged students to do better than their best, which Hazo insists "is what the pursuit of excellence means." A complete disregard for university bureaucracy was one of the qualities Hazo admired most about O'Malley, who never relinquished his belief that an intellectual and spiritual agenda must guide the decisions of the university administration. O'Malley believed students, too, must embrace this intellectual and spiritual agenda instead of concerning themselves merely with an accumulation of credits. O'Malley was "far from the most sociable man in the world," Hazo says. "If you forgot your text or your notebook, he would say crisply 'Why didn't you forget your lungs?'" (*Outspokenly Yours*, 29), but he had a brilliant mind and was universally recognized as an excellent professor. Hazo relates the following story in an essay titled "To Teach, Perchance to Learn":

When he [Frank O'Malley] died, he was laid in state in front of his classroom. After the funeral, his family and friends went to his bachelor's room on campus to look for "the big book" he had been rumored to be working on. Instead, they found on one side of his bed all the books his former students had published. (Edwin O'Connor dedicated *The Last Hurrah* to him.) On the other side of the bed were the best papers his students had written over five decades. And under the bed was a shoebox filled with uncashed checks—repayments that students had sent to him for "loans" he had made to them when they needed the money. (*Outspokenly Yours*, 29)

Perhaps the truest testimony to O'Malley's greatness as a teacher occurred twenty-four years after his death, when former students packed a memorial in his honor. "Teaching meant everything to him, and we all knew it," Hazo explains. "Students and learning constituted his life."

The Philosophy of Literature sequence, and indeed the entirety of his four years at Notre Dame, had a profound impact on Hazo's worldview and future profession. As literature, philosophy, and theology began to develop greater significance in his intellectual life, law school lost its appeal. In his journal, Hazo says, "Notre Dame to me meant finding myself. Without that experience, I would not be doing what I'm doing now."

In fact, the Philosophy of Literature course first introduced Hazo to the works of French philosopher Jacques Maritain, who wrote extensively on aesthetics. Maritain's influence on the development of Hazo's own ideas about art was so significant that Maritain became the subject of Hazo's dissertation, "The World within the Word: Maritain and the Poet" (University of Pittsburgh, 1957). The dissertation, which analyzes Maritain's philosophies on aesthetics through the lens of several English poets whom Hazo most admires—namely, Gerard Manley Hopkins, John Keats, and Samuel Taylor Coleridge—became the foundation for Hazo's own poetic aesthetic. Although his philosophical theories on art developed greater depth and complexity over the years as he continued to write both poetry and prose, Hazo's basic ideologies never strayed from those outlined in his dissertation.

Sixty-one years after he wrote the dissertation, it was published by Franciscan University Press with an introduction written by James Matthew Wilson, a Maritain scholar whose views were also profoundly influenced by his undergraduate education at the University of Notre Dame. Wilson says:

Our intellectual lives were shaped by Notre Dame and what it can offer. The singular representative of that offering is Jacques Maritain,
the modern philosopher who showed us if we think about the world in
terms of being, of reality, there is no aspect of that world that is outside our concern or fragmented and broken away from the totality of
wisdom... I always would have enjoyed [Hazo's] poetry, but seeing how
directly its concern for the straight voice derives from what Maritain described as a concern for the *real*, for the encounter with the act of being
that metaphysics describes by way of abstraction, but to which works of
art give us a kind of existential access—seeing that helped me also to see
how marvelously Hazo makes the simple, the unadorned, the colloquial,
a means to enter into the mystery of reality. His mode of association in
his poetry captures the way in which odd and unanticipated meanings
hide in everyday objects. (interview, January 18, 2019)

Like most college students, Hazo benefited from more than
just the curriculum during those formative years at Notre Dame.
He recalls his part-time job, a 1947 national debating championship, a few extraordinary classmates, and a beautiful girlfriend
named Yvonne as significant contributors to his college experience. And, of course, the discovery of every college student's favorite food: pizza.

Hazo's four-year scholarship made a college degree possible, but it did not cover all of the costs related to attending a
university. To pay those additional expenses, Hazo held various
part-time jobs close to campus—including one position working
in the priests' dining room in Corby Hall. Despite the various
employment, however, Hazo recalls having almost no spending
money for those four years. He even did all of his own laundry
in his dorm room to save some money. The pennies that Hazo
saved by hand-washing his clothes and hanging them to dry were
put to various good and practical uses. One of the few things he
allowed himself to splurge on once or twice a month was a large
pizza (which cost fifty cents) at a pizzeria close to campus. Hazo
had never tasted pizza before college because it was not yet com-

mon fare in the 1940s. But once he tried it, he knew it was worth saving for! The owners of the tiny pizza shop were a newly married couple, and apparently Hazo was not the only one who got hooked on their pizza. Their tiny "mom and pop" shop, according to Hazo, is now a large pizzeria and restaurant that occupies the better part of a city block.

In his senior year, Hazo met Mary Katherine Yvonne Rauch, the daughter of his Philosophy of Literature professor, Rufus Rauch. "We went on dates, fell for each other, and became what you would call 'sweethearts' in my senior year and for a short time after graduation," Hazo recalls in his journal. "We were serious." When Hazo moved back to Pittsburgh after graduation and started working as a reporter for the *Pittsburgh Post-Gazette*, he and Yvonne stayed in touch through letters. Yvonne even visited Hazo in Pittsburgh, staying with Aunt Katherine and him for a week. "She was quite beautiful," Hazo remembers, "but we were also quite young—just around twenty." Hazo admits he realized even then that, although they got along wonderfully, the romance wouldn't last. "It was too ill-timed to have the time to mature." Hazo did not take any action to end the relationship, but he also didn't work to maintain it, thinking in his twenty-year-old male mind that "These things just take care of themselves." One day, Yvonne returned a bracelet Hazo had given her—via the Postal Service—with no note. "That was the end of it," Hazo said. A few years later, he learned from Yvonne's brother that she was getting married (Journal).

Regardless of how amazing your college classes and girlfriends are, most would agree that the extracurricular experiences shared with your friends create some of the best and most enduring memories. Hazo vividly remembers many of his Notre Dame classmates, some of whom he has maintained friendships with over the years.

First there was John Grimes, a former marine from Alabama

and Hazo's best friend in college. Hazo recalls that John wanted nothing more than to join his brother in the Diplomatic Courier Service after graduation. He found success in the courier service shortly after graduating and insisted that he had no intention of marrying anyone for years to come. Less than one year later, however, John married Sylvia, a young Egyptian Jewish woman who was born in Cairo. She and John had three children and lived in Arlington, Virginia.

Hazo remembers his friend Jim Klockenkemper as a young man who was always smiling. A middleweight boxer, Jim invited Hazo to spar with him one day. The memory makes Hazo chuckle: "He boxed the ears off me, knocked me out of the ring, and could have finished me off anytime he wanted." Instead, he told Hazo they had sparred long enough, assured him that he was "not bad," and smiled his unforgettable smile. Twenty years later, Hazo recalls, he was killed in a tragic automobile accident, leaving a wife and children to mourn his loss.

Frank Finn was Hazo's brilliant debate partner at Notre Dame in 1947—the year they won the national debating championship. He became a prominent lawyer in Dallas and had three sons and a daughter.

Johnny Lujack was an irrepressible all-American quarterback from Connellsville, Pennsylvania. He never quarterbacked a losing game at Notre Dame and won the Heisman Trophy in 1947. The consummate athlete, Johnny also played on the varsity softball team with Hazo one summer. Hazo remembers that Johnny could "throw a ball in a straight line from deep left field directly to the catcher."

A few other classmates worthy of mention included José Napoleon Duarte, who later became the president of El Salvador; Bill Pfaff, who became a successful author and syndicated columnist for the *International Herald Tribune*; Tom Dooley, who left the lucrative medical profession he established to become a missionary doctor in Asia; and Pete Ahrens, who ran a successful Oldsmobile dealership in Madison, Wisconsin, and whose sister was the head of the Maryknoll Order of nuns. And then there was Pete Dachbach, a calm, soft-spoken naval cadet at Notre Dame who took his own life years after graduating "for reasons no one can name." These were the names and faces of classmates who added immeasurable joy and countless memorable experiences to Hazo's undergraduate education at Notre Dame. They were friends and classmates he would never forget.

Hazo made his initial foray into writing poetry while attending Notre Dame. Although he considers most of what he wrote there "a lot of junk" (Furlong, 5), the short poem "Diminuendo" survived the test of time. Published in Hazo's very first volume of poetry, *Discovery and Other Poems* (1959), the poem was also included in his much later collection *Once for the Last Bandit* (1972). Hazo rounded out his successful undergraduate career at Notre Dame by winning the James V. Mitchell Award for Playwriting in his senior year, and he graduated magna cum laude in 1948—when he was just nineteen years old.

Dr. Leo O'Donnell remained Sam Hazo's patron for the full four years. Hazo truly appreciates Dr. O'Donnell's role in setting the course for what would become a successful, fulfilling, and beautiful life. Hazo says, "Notre Dame played such a central part in my life. Without Notre Dame, where would I be?" He adds:

It has been said that our projected life span can be divided into thirds: one third schooling; one third sleeping; one third earning. Most people conceive of the last third as the most important, but it strikes me that the first third is. How you do in the first third actually determines the direction of the last third. And the second third can't be taken for granted either. If you have trouble sleeping, you can't do anything well. So there you have it: learning, sleeping, earning. And learning is king. (Journal)

The importance of Hazo's time at Notre Dame is clear in two poems about return visits to the university for special occasions. He wrote "Breakfasting with Sophomores" after accepting an invitation to give a poetry reading at a sophomore literary festival in 1973—and yes, he actually had breakfast with the students. In the poem, Hazo ponders the significance of perspective as we age. For college students with a lifetime ahead of them, the future holds all the beautiful promise of their hopes and dreams. Equipped with the knowledge gained twenty-five years after graduation, however, nothing is more important to the poet than everything that is happening right now:

Breakfasting with Sophomores

When I was what you are, the world
   was every place I'd yet to go.
Nothing near, now, or here
   meant more than something anywhere
   tomorrow.
           Today, the ratio's reversed.
Back from anywhere, I watch
   the Indiana earth I walked,
   measure Indiana's level weathers
   and remember ...
           Where did twenty-five
   Decembers go?
         North of action,
   east of indecision, south
   of possibility, and west of hope,
   I stare into the now and then
   of all those years at once.
A sophomore who has my name jogs
   by in ski boots and an army-surplus
   jacket.

Netless tennis courts
turn populous with players only
I can recognize.
        Oblivious,
the campus pines still celebrate
their rooted anniversaries.
                        A DC-7
seams the zenith with a chalkmark
wake, and clouds rush over
lake, dome, and stadium
like bursts of smoke from field
artillery ...
                No different in its bones,
no greener, not a foot more hilly,
Indiana's real for the acknowledging.
I sit back, listening, observing,
memorizing everything.
Two decades' worth
of meals and months and mileage
consecrates this minute.
                        Even
an eyelash swimming in my coffee
seems important.
                When I was half
my age, I never would have seen it.

Hazo wrote "Notre Dame du Lac" in 1998, after returning
for his fiftieth class reunion. It was the only reunion Hazo attended, and he went solely because his wife Mary Anne wanted
to. Although Mary Anne did not attend Notre Dame, "she loved
it more than I did," Hazo says. Several hundred classmates and
their spouses attended the reunion, which surprised Hazo. He
also recalled that he thoroughly enjoyed it—which, he confesses,
surprised him even more. In this poem, the Notre Dame campus

with its iconic landmarks bears witness to the importance of the past, the present, and the future:

Notre Dame du Lac

1

Everywhere the same campus trees—
    fifty autumns thicker, taller
    and scheduled to sleeve their naked
    bark in January's ermine.
A male and female cardinal
    peck at huckleberries on a limb.
Paired for life, they beak
    each berry as their last and first.
Sparrows cling to branches,
    wires, sheer brick walls,
    anything where they can roost.
A chipmunk scoots and pauses
    by the numbers.
                Unlike all peacock
    prancers on parade or the zombie
    stomp of soldiery, backpacking
    students cycle, rollerblade
    and stroll to their different drummers.
They pass like Giacometti's
    striders—eyes full front
    but aimed at destinations still
    within themselves …
                  Beyond
    Nantucket a jet's about to crash.
Bradley's challenging Gore.
Ted Hesburgh's fit and eighty-two
    with one good eye.

"May I
serve God better with one eye
than I did with two."
                    Seated
behind me at a football game,
a woman from Dallas tells me
her Pittsburgh mother had an uncle—
Leo O'Donnell, a doctor.
                              She knows
I've flown from Pittsburgh for the day.
Eighty thousand cheer around us.
"O'Donnell," she repeats.
                        I swallow
and say that Dr. O'Donnell funded
"my scholarship to study here"
a half-century back.
                        The odds
are eighty thousand plus to one
that I should meet his Texas niece
today in this crammed stadium
in Indiana, but I do.
                        What else
is there to say?
                    It's now
all over the world.
                    Everything's
happening.
            Anything can happen.

                    2
We've journeyed back to grass
    and souvenirs and beige bricks.
The sky's exactly the same.

Acre by acre, the campus
  widens like a stage designed
  for a new play.
            Why
  do we gawk like foreigners
  at residence halls no longer
  ours but somehow ours
  in perpetuity?
            We visit them
  like their alumni—older
  but unchanged.
                Half a century
  of students intervenes.
                    They stroll
  among us now, invisible
  but present as the air before
  they fade and disappear.
                    It's like
  the day we swam at St. Joseph's
  Lake.
            We churned the surface
  into suds with every stroke and kick.
After we crossed, the water
  stilled and settled to a sheen
  as if we never swam at all.
One memory was all we kept
  to prove we'd been together
  in that very lake, and swimming.
Each time we tell this story,
  someone says we're living out
  a dream.

We say we're only
reuniting with the lives
we lived.
As long as we
can say they were, they *were* . . .
And what they were, we are.

In this poem, current students "stroll to their different drum-mers," yet unfazed by future events and tragedies, and perhaps not fully grasping the importance of the present moment. These students fade into memories of the poet's own experiences at the university fifty years previously, recollections engrained in his mind not through pictures and videos on social media, but as sto-ries he has shared throughout the years—memories that helped to shape the man he has become. Commenting on the poem, James Matthew Wilson says, "'Notre Dame du Lac' captures so well what Sam and I have in common: a sense that Catholic uni-versity education makes possible a kind of intellectual flourish-ing that would be unavailable otherwise, and that this in turn is founded on the charity of others" (interview, January 18, 2019).

As a tribute to his alma mater and an incentive to young po-ets, Hazo established the Samuel and Mary Anne Hazo Poetry Award, a five-hundred-dollar prize given annually to a promising undergraduate student writer at Notre Dame. In 2008, as recog-nition of his outstanding contributions to the literary arts, the university awarded Hazo an honorary degree—a doctor of hu-mane letters—his tenth of twelve honorary degrees to date.

THREE

Transition

There is no word for what I love in you
but it is sure, sacred, and daily as bread.

"For My Last Class of Freshmen"

It's usually easier to follow the thread of our life and career choices in retrospect than when struggling in the moment to make important decisions. For Hazo, it would seem his life must have always been on a trajectory toward writing and teaching. But that's not how the arc of his life came to light. As with so many of us, we take opportunities as they arise, assume a let's-see attitude toward whether or not the choice is a good fit, find that coincidences and events come to bear on our situations, and, with luck, eventually find our niche. The transitions Hazo experienced along his journey gave him wisdom and understanding that he drew upon when he finally found his calling in education and writing.

After graduating from the University of Note Dame in 1948, Hazo moved back home with Aunt Katherine. Because he was so young (only twenty), it was difficult to find a position commensurate with his education. He worked briefly as a truck loader for the Squirt Bottling Company before securing a position as a reporter for the *Pittsburgh Post-Gazette*. He and his editor quickly realized, however, that journalism was not for him. "I did not enjoy the work," Hazo remembers, "and my editor must not have enjoyed my work either because one day when I arrived at the office, he told me I was through." Feeling utterly confused about what he wanted to do with his life, Hazo took a job as a laborer on a farm for almost a year. And then came Korea.

When the Korean War began in 1950, the threat of being drafted was very real to the healthy twenty-two-year-old Hazo. Realizing that he would have to serve wherever the government placed him if drafted, Hazo decided to enlist voluntarily. He began with a visit to the US Air Force recruitment office. As a college graduate, he was offered a commission with the air force, which meant that he would be starting his service as an officer. Despite the appealing nature of a commission, though, Hazo decided he just wasn't fond of the air force. He remembered a number of marines whom he had met and liked at Notre Dame, so he decided to visit their recruitment office next. Unlike the air force, the marines offered commissions only to college graduates who had served in the ROTC, which Hazo had not. Nevertheless, he decided he liked the marines and enlisted as a private for a four-year term.

Hazo vividly remembers the morning that he left for boot camp at Parris Island in Beaufort, South Carolina, particularly how brave and lonely Aunt Katherine looked when he left her at the streetcar stop on her way to work. With Robert at St. John's College in Maryland and Hazo in the marines, Aunt Katherine would be alone for the first time. Although she was healthy and vibrant, Hazo still felt concerned about her solitary living situation.

Life as a Vow

She'd made a deathbed promise
to our mother to raise the two
of us.

She never broke it.
Not for marriage, money,
or other options ...
                    Later,
when my brother and I were
off to college or in the service,
she lived alone for seven
years, trolleying to work
and back, grocering en route
and cooking for herself
by herself.
                    For fifty-seven
months she worked and lived
like that so we would know
that home was there and waiting.
That's called devotion.
                    Otherwise,
she judged a woman by how
she dressed and carried herself
in public.
                    Once at a funeral home,
a woman in a black dress
and black hose asked her, "Katherine,
how old are you now?"
                    Without
a pause, she answered, Ninety-seven."
The woman gasped, "Katherine,
you don't look it!"
                    After
we left, I asked her, "Why
did you say you were ninety-seven
when you're really sixty?"

                                              "She
wanted me to be ninety-seven."
Of all women, the only ones
    she admired were our mother
    and her sister-in-law.
                                  "It takes
    a good woman to live
    with my brother."
                            Among
    my memories, the one that lasts
    is the morning I left for Parris
    Island.
                    We waited for our trolleys
    together.
                    Mine came first.
We kissed.
                    After I boarded,
    I looked back and saw her standing
    so alone, so utterly alone.

Like all recruits, Hazo experienced long and physically challenging days in boot camp. Training started at six o'clock each
morning, ended after many hours of physical exertion, and was
usually punctuated by guard duty at night. Fortunately, Hazo was
in good physical condition, so he did not experience any prob-
lems or setbacks. After several months, Hazo received orders to
report to an aircraft engineering squadron in Quantico, Virginia,
where he was assigned because of his typing skills. His adminis-
trative skills served him well for another few months in Quantico, during which time he took as many weekend opportunities as
possible to visit his brother Robert at St. John's College.

Finally, the Marine Corps opened an officer's program for
enlisted men with a college degree, and Hazo applied. Five hundred men were accepted into the program along with Hazo, and

they all came together for a rigorous eight-week officers' screening program at Quantico. When the screening ended, Hazo was among the two hundred men who were selected to be commissioned as marine officers; the other three hundred were told to report to their previous duties. Platoon leaders' training began the very next day at Camp Barrett, and "Oddly enough," Hazo says, "I remember very little about this four-month segment of my military service. I do recall that there were graduates from many different universities throughout the country in the program—some of whom went on to serve in Korea and elsewhere." At the end of the training, the men were gathered together to receive their orders. After all the orders had been given, five men—including Hazo—were still sitting there. Apparently, orders had not yet been cut for them, and they were told to remain on base until their orders came in. As a result, he and the other four marines spent a leisurely five days on an essentially deserted base that had been bustling with the activity of two hundred men just days prior.

Commissioned as a second lieutenant with a new contract to serve for two years active duty and five years in the Marine Reserve, Hazo finally received his assignment: "My luck was to serve as a paymaster ('disbursement officer' was the military term) in Portsmouth, Virginia. I was stationed at a Marine Corps Forwarding Depot; we forwarded supplies and so forth to marines in the Atlantic and Mediterranean. I was then promoted to first lieutenant. And after that, I served as a legal officer in Portsmouth dealing with court martials and things like that." Hazo laughs when he remembers his service as a legal officer. "Can you imagine that?" he asks.

During this period in Portsmouth, Hazo lived off base with a local family because there was no room for the new officers on the base. He bought his first car for transportation between the base and his residence and "lived a rather lonely life—interrupt-

SAM HAZO, UNITED STATES MARINE CORPS, CHRISTMAS 1952

ed now and then with visits to St. John's College or trips back to Pittsburgh."

Hazo's first experience resisting a truly racist authority figure also occurred during his service as an officer. The colonel in charge of Hazo's unit knew that Hazo had graduated from Notre Dame—home of the Fighting Irish football team. Although Hazo had never played college football, his colonel asked him to put together a football team on the base. Hazo complied, and the new team lost five of the six games that season to various army and navy teams. Feeling pretty good about the one win—which happened to be the last game of the season—Hazo asked if they could give the men a banquet to celebrate. The colonel agreed and even gave permission for the banquet to be held in the Officers' Club—as long as Hazo made sure the Black players knew they were not invited. Hazo respectfully told the colonel that he would not agree to plan a banquet under those circumstances, and he certainly wouldn't attend one. After that exchange, the colonel asked the white players on the team—composed of privates, corporals, sergeants, and the like—to plan the banquet. In a beautiful demonstration of solidarity, they all turned him down. "So we did not have the banquet," Hazo reports. It was then he learned an important lesson about the repercussions of defying authority in the name of justice: "I was subsequently relieved of my duties as a legal officer, and I spent the next month before I was discharged just vegetating. He didn't give me anything to do. That was his way of getting even. The day I was supposed to leave, I went in at 8:00 a.m. to get my separation orders, and he made me wait until two o'clock in the afternoon before he gave them to me."

Hazo could not have known it at the time, but that bigoted and vengeful colonel actually contributed to what would become a successful writing career for the young Sam Hazo. The month he spent "vegetating"—that is, not engaged in any physical work—turned out to be time well spent, as he turned inward to the world of the mind. Hazo had been experimenting with poetry here and there because, as he explains, "If you're in the service and you don't keep your mind alive, it's a long way down." The military does not generally provide much time for contemplation, however, so he had not attempted much serious writing. The punishment of inactivity while he waited for his separation orders therefore allowed him the time and space necessary to focus on writing—and he enjoyed it. "If you don't keep your mind alive, you're just living according to orders, and that's no life. That's the life of a slave." In a 2004 interview for *Pitt Magazine*, Hazo said, "I began writing just as a way to keep my sanity. And I've been doing it ever since for the same reason" ("Poetic Justice," 6).

Home in Pittsburgh after two and a half years of active military service, Hazo lived the life of a reservist—attending meetings every Thursday night and completing a two-week tour of duty in the summers. He married Mary Anne and was promoted to captain, and his only real concern was the possibility of being recalled for active duty and sent to a war zone. In retrospect, Hazo is thankful he was never deployed to Korea. While he was on active duty, however, he would have been willing to serve. "People that I knew were there—men I served with. As a matter of fact, one time I even wrote a letter requesting to go. I had bought into the whole military ideology while I was a marine. But the colonel called me in and said, 'You've got a good deal here, Hazo. Just stay where you are.'"

Recalling his military service after more than sixty years as a civilian, Hazo says that his time in the Marine Corps seems like a dream to him now. He remembers maintaining many military habits for years after he left the marines: keeping in step with people walking on the sidewalk and wearing his military underwear until they wore out, for example. "You do it for several years," Hazo says, "and it leaves a mark on how you conduct your daily affairs. After a time, of course, you begin to see these habits for what they are, and they gradually wear away."

Written before their fiftieth reunion in 2003, "Toasts for the Lost Lieutenants" is a tribute to some of the men with whom Hazo served.

Toasts for the Lost Lieutenants

For Karl the Cornell rower,
    who wore the medals he deserved.
For Grogan of Brooklyn, who left
    no memory worth mentioning.
For Foley, who married the commandant's
    daughter though nothing came of it.
For Clasby, who wanted out,
    and when he could, got out.
For Schoen, who married, stayed in,
    thickened, and retired a major.
For Chalfant, who bought a sword
    and dress blues but remained Chalfant.
For Billy Adrian, the best
    of punters, legless in Korea.
For Nick Christopolos, who kept
    a luger just in case.
For Soderbergh, who taught us
    songs on hot Sundays.
For Dahlstrom, the tennis king,
    who starched his dungarees erect.
For Jacobson, who followed me
    across the worst of all creeks.
For Laffin and the gun he cracked
    against a rock and left there.
For Nathan Hale, who really was
    descended but shrugged it off.

For Elmore, buried in Yonkers
    five presidents ago.
For Lonnie MacMillan, who spoke
    his Alabamian mind regardless.
For Bremser of Yale, who had *it*
    and would always have *it*.
For lean Clyde Lee, who stole
    from Uncle once too often.
For Dewey Ehling and the clarinet
    he kept but never played.
For Lockett of the Sugar Bowl
    champs, and long may he run.
For Lyle Beeler, may he rot
    as an aide to the aide of an aide.
For Joe Buergler, who never
    would pitch in the majors.
For Kerg, who called all women cows
    but married one who wasn't.
For me, who flunked each
    test on weapons but the last.
For Sheridan, who flunked them all,
    then goofed the battle games
    by leaving his position, hiding
    in a pine above the generals'
    latrine until he potted
    every general in sight, thus
    stopping single-handedly the war.

Hazo enjoyed reuniting with many of these men in 2003. The first marine mentioned in the poem—"Karl the Cornell rower"— became the athletic director at the Naval Academy in Annapolis and then at West Point. Peter Soderbergh, who loved music and "taught us songs on hot Sundays," became a professor and dean of the College of Education at Louisiana State University. He also passed his love for music and theater on to his son, Steven Soderbergh, who became a successful director, screenwriter, and producer.

George "Bremser of Yale, who had *it* / and would always have *it*" was an exemplary marine with whom Hazo maintained a lifelong friendship. After his first marriage ended, George remained single for quite a long time. Waiting for a friend at the opera one evening, George struck up a conversation with a woman who was also waiting for a friend to arrive. As the curtain time approached, it became clear that neither friend was going to show up, so George took a chance: "Would you like to see the opera with me?" he asked. "I have two very good seats." She agreed, and they had a nice evening together. He called her the next week to tell her that he enjoyed her company and to invite her to lunch, but the woman who answered the phone said, "She doesn't want to speak with you." He was stunned and didn't understand why she would not speak with him after their lovely experience at the opera. About a month later, he tore his Achilles tendon after a fall, and was laid up with nothing to do. She was still on his mind, so he decided to call her again, and the same woman answered. He explained where they had met and that he would just like to tell her how much he enjoyed her company. Finally, the woman on the phone told him what had happened: his new friend had been helping one of her sister's children get out of a swimming pool, and she ruptured something in her spine. She could no longer walk, and the paraplegia would be permanent. He responded with, "Well, we're even now. I can't walk because I have a torn tendon." So she invited him over, they began a beautiful relationship, and they ended up getting married. Only three years later, however, she died of pneumonia. When Hazo saw George at the fiftieth reunion, she had just died a few months previously. Hazo says, "He was there, but I could see that he was a haunted man."

Hazo wrote "Mustangs"—a term used to describe an enlisted

man who becomes an officer—after visiting with his former classmates at their fiftieth reunion. "We were 5th Special Basic Class: the only class that's memorialized at Camp Barrett in Quantico, Virginia," Hazo says. A memorial engraved with all of their names was erected in their honor and unveiled at the reunion because they were the first class of enlisted men who were commissioned as officers in the marines at Camp Barrett.

Mustangs

5th Special Basic Class, US Marine Corps

Older by fifty years,
    we grouped for photographs beside
    apartment BOQ's that once
    were Quonset huts.
                The new
    lieutenants held us in embarrassing
    esteem.
            Of some three hundred
    in our old battalion, three
    were killed in combat, and the rest
    lived on to die of the usual
    or simply to survive and re-unite.
Necklaced with tags to prove
    we were who we were, we met
    without bravado.
              Grandfathers mostly,
    we drank black coffee like alumni
    and avoided politics.
             Two days
    together placed us squarely
    in our generation.

                    No one pretended
    to be other than himself.
                            We parted
    as we parted half a century
    before, uncertain when or where
    we'd meet again.
                    Or if.

Overall, Hazo benefited from his military experience: "I met
all kinds of men—from heroes to scoundrels. I was given the G.I.
Bill of Rights, which permitted me to go to graduate school and
acquire an MA and PhD. And I learned to work under distracting
conditions and not be distracted from whatever I was doing. I
can't overestimate the value of those benefits." Even before he
joined, however, Hazo realized that the structure of the military
would be problematic because he knew that he could never think
only in terms of rank or seniority, he could never see human beings as merely "personnel," and he could never accept the habit of
mind where strict obedience is the rule: "As one to whom obedience to one's conscience is the ultimate loyalty, I have a guarded
skepticism about blind obedience to superiors, whether the setting be military, governmental, ecclesiastical, commercial, or academic" ("When Clocks Have No Hands"). Despite this inherent
skepticism, however, Hazo knew that from 1950 to 1957, he would
have to deal with it—and he did just that.

    There's a significant difference between "dealing" and "thriv-
ing," though, and Hazo knew that in order to thrive, he needed to
satisfy his mind, heart, and soul. After the marines, therefore, he
would need to establish himself outside of any large bureaucracy
where rank replaces intelligence, and people become personnel.
"This is one reason I have always admired education, where intelligence is recognized and encouraged and rewarded—for the
most part—regardless of race, creed, sex, or age. It creates a

standard where human beings can grow and not just be bossed around. People become *real* people when they live in such an atmosphere of freedom and are not just so many economic slaves." For Hazo, there is simply "no substitute for intellectual freedom and the exercise thereof" ("When Clocks Have No Hands").

Returning from the Marine Corps, Hazo worked at a summer camp for boys in Greenville, Pennsylvania. He received an offer to work for Harcourt Brace book publishers, but opted instead to earn advanced degrees under the G.I. Bill and become a teacher. "I decided it was better to get what was in books into the heads of students rather than to market or edit books for teachers to use," Hazo explains. "I've never regretted that decision." Looking back, Hazo contemplates the reasons that teaching seemed to suggest itself. "Perhaps it had to do with the lifestyle of several teachers I admired at Notre Dame. Perhaps it may even go back to the fact that my mother was a teacher, teaching English to immigrant children in the Epiphany Grade School."

After his stint as a camp counselor, Hazo accepted a teaching position at Pittsburgh's Shady Side Academy, which was a private all-boys boarding school at the time. He also started taking graduate courses at night and on Saturdays at Duquesne University, and he maintained his obligation as a reserve officer, reporting for duty every Thursday evening and for two weeks of summer training at Camp Lejeune, North Carolina.

Teaching at Shady Side Academy was an adventure for Hazo. He taught English, Latin, Spanish, and mathematics and also coached the basketball and baseball teams—"all on a grand salary of $3,000.00 per year!" He explains that this income would have been sufficient if he lived on campus, where meals and an apartment were provided for instructors and their families. But since he was living with Kak, the administration did not feel inclined to make him the offer. "They also didn't offer me the difference in salary," Hazo says, "so I was gotten 'on the cheap.'"

SAM HAZO PLAYING FOOTBALL WITH STUDENTS AT SHADY SIDE ACADEMY,
CIRCA 1954

Despite the low pay, Hazo thoroughly enjoyed teaching the young men at Shady Side Academy. He kept the position for two years while earning his graduate degree, and over the summer of his second year there, married his beloved Mary Anne. After completing his master's degree at Duquesne University in 1955, Hazo accepted a full-time teaching position at Duquesne, where he taught fifteen credit hours per semester, started the doctoral program at the University of Pittsburgh, and taught an extra course at Carnegie Institute of Technology (now Carnegie Mellon University) in the evenings.

When asked what he learned from his years of long hours and low wages in his twenties, he says, "I learned how to work hard, that's for sure, and I learned how to discipline myself and not waste time. And I most definitely learned that employers take total advantage of young people who are just starting out. Looking back on those days, I wonder how in God's name I did what I did."

The poem "Transition" traces Hazo's metamorphosis from marine lieutenant to Latin teacher. While seemingly counterintuitive, the progression from physical battleground to intellectual front lines is a more logical evolution than one may initially realize.

Transition

A collar weighted with lieutenant's bars
made this a face to be saluted once
and possibly despised by one platoon
I marched ten miles in Norfolk Fahrenheit.
Close-order-drill made me the martinet
I tried to tame, but Adam in my blood
inclined to epaulets until each stance
and striding flexed my sinews for command.

Soft holsters felt familiar at my hip,
and bayonets drove easily through groins
of dummies gallowed for the practice thrusts
like snakes impaled and twisting on a tine
to ready me for months of counting cash.
Released, I paid myself my vouchered sum
with bills that curved my wallet like a stave
and drove the pre-paid mileage into days

of typing theses in quintuplicate
and teaching boys the Latin ablative.
Surrendering my barracked ways meant more
than wearing out my military socks.

I kept a wry reservist's look for half
a year and still keep step with walkers-by,
although I hate the spectacle of squads
paced to a cadence in a drummed parade.

Between the sweep and sudden cease of grace
I wage today the quiet wars of art
with students calmly primed to probe my views
in lectures I cannot pre-think or plan.
I tell them only what I right now know.
I ask them only what they right now see
and take some triumph from each day's defeat
in my and everybody's war and peace.

Although the transition from marine lieutenant to teacher occurs seamlessly mid-stanza: "Released, I paid myself my vouchered sum / with bills that curved my wallet like a stave / and drove the pre-paid mileage into days / of typing theses in quintuplicate / and teaching boys the Latin ablative," the reader soon realizes that the poet holds a deep-seated ambivalence about his military service. As a marine, his rank as lieutenant at once commands respect from others and weighs on him emotionally. He is a strict disciplinarian who yearns to command and can easily thrust a bayonet through the groins of practice dummies, and yet he feels like the one "impaled and twisting on a tine" until ultimately being released from the service. Once he begins to live his new life as a teacher, he struggles to shed his military ways because they have become so deeply ingrained in his psyche: "Surrendering my barracked ways meant more / than wearing out my military socks. / I kept a wry reservist's look for half / a year." And although he detests the blind conformity of military practices, he can't help "keep[ing] step with walkers-by." Not until the final stanza does the lieutenant-turned-teacher find comfort and real satisfaction in his new role. Here he realizes that, as a teacher, he is shepherding his students through complex intellectual battle-fields: waging "quiet wars of art" and experiencing daily triumphs and defeats as they fight to become educated.

Preparing young people to navigate life's complexities through education suited Hazo perfectly. The position he accept-ed at Duquesne in 1955 remained his until 1998, when he retired after forty-three years of service. During that time, he earned a PhD from the University of Pittsburgh (1957); published his first book of poems, *Discovery and Other Poems* (1958); published three plays and thirty-four additional books of poetry, fiction, and scholarship; founded and directed the International Poetry Fo-rum (which will be discussed at length in chapter 5); and enjoyed promotions through the ranked faculty to tenured full professor. He even served as associate dean of the College of Arts and Sci-ences for three years—a position he did not enjoy.

To Hazo, teaching is more than a mere job—"it's truly a call-ing, a vocation. It's an invitation that really can't be refused, and it transcends all the paperwork or committee work that goes with it." Like many of us who remember and appreciate the teachers who inspired us, Hazo owes his love of books and passion for teaching to several outstanding professors he had at the Univer-sity of Notre Dame. Exemplary teachers invariably continue to influence their students far beyond the classroom. "Theirs is a treasure of a legacy," Hazo says. In the essay titled "To Teach, Per-chance to Learn," Hazo expounds upon this idea:

When asked what America stands for, we do not talk about insider trad-ing, chicanery in public life, greed in the marketplace, gangs and drive-by shootings, the prolonged juvenilia of many professional athletes or even what is called the two-party system. We ultimately talk about those val-ues that are fostered in public and private education. Teachers are the ones who do that fostering. Those who think that this fostering is not primarily important and worthy of sacrifice and support need only imag-ine what the country would be like without them. (*Outspokenly Yours*, 29)

When Hazo began his collegiate teaching career at Duquesne, his greatest satisfaction was discovering that teaching is not mere *instruction*. It is, on the contrary, an act of love: "It's sharing not just what you know but what you don't know. It's sharing a spirit of learning with somebody, as opposed to those people who think that a teacher is somebody who knows it all and shares it with somebody who knows nothing. There's a myth for you. It's not just a myth, it's a lie. Teachers are just older students" (Hazo qtd. in Sokolowski, 255). For Hazo, teaching involves studying, discussing, debating, and pursuing a subject, a poem, a novel, whatever it happens to be, fervidly until you find a satisfactory meaning, solution, answer, or response. "Sometimes an insight just comes to you when you least expect it and you can't even take credit for it," Hazo asserts. "But it's true and you can't deny it." The following poem illustrates this exquisite phenomenon, ultimately acknowledging it as divine inspiration:

Open Letter to a Closed Mind

I make too much of it, this matter of books
and talk and silences, but every sun
I stand less sure of what I ought to know
and find my way to them to find my way.
Wisdom's rabbit races just far enough
ahead to keep the chase invitingly close
but never done, and all I really know
is what occurs to me right here as right.
Moments of truth come anywhere at once.

Facing the jewelry of bottles twiced
by mirrors fanned behind a downtown bar
in Minneapolis, I understood a verse
from Crane's *The Wine Menagerie* without
intending it. The meaning simply *came*,

like *that*—like one of God's gratuities
that come before we are prepared. Of all
I ever worked to learn, those things are best
that came without my earning them.

I should have said without *deserving* them.
In Minneapolis a deeper thinker
surely would have called all truth a gift,
but it was hot, and I forgot. Later,
when students let me tell them what I knew,
I saw that all we keep of truth is what
we give away, that holocausts can sleep
like revolutions in the smallest flints,
that any river can reflect the sun.

I have a student's fear that truth is fun
to seek but death to keep. Heroes and saints
are those who freed the thoughts of God by pen
or tongue and made them last like Parthenons.
I bleed the lambs of glory for those few
who said that time must wait their christening.
In the presence of their absence, words take flesh,
and God wakes fires that can rock the skull
and blaze the eye with revelation.

The power of this poem builds gradually—starting with the
poet's daily uncertainty about his own knowledge, to moments
of insight and truth-sharing, and ultimately to the gift of divine
inspiration. The message: truth is holy, and those who seek it will
be rewarded.

Hazo's students have been a source of great joy in his life. In
class or after class, teaching and learning were reciprocal because
"students have insights and ideas that we might never see without them." One example of this occurred many years ago yet remains fresh in Hazo's memory. He recounts the story:

There was a student named Eric Kloss in my Introduction to Literature course. He was a great jazz saxophonist, and he was blind. In class we were studying "Love and a Question" by Robert Frost. In the poem, a man and his new bride are alone in their home. He is putting wood on the fire and she's eagerly waiting for him in anticipation of an amorous evening. There's a knock on the door; he answers it and there's a beggar standing there. It's snowing like hell and it's cold. It's his wedding night. And that's where the poem ends. So I asked the class, "What effect does this poem have on you? What should the bridegroom do?" The women said, "You have to take him in. It's snowing and he has nothing." The men said, "Give him some money and tell him to shove off." Eric was sitting quietly, listening to the discussion. I said "Eric, what do you think?" He paused for a moment, and then he said, "It's no good. He's there, man." In that one comment, Eric essentially rendered our entire conversation moot. It doesn't matter what the bride and groom were preparing for because suddenly life intervened and you can't act as if it didn't happen.

"He's there, man."

For Hazo, this is the kind of casual aside where real learning happens, for both students and teachers. It's not the course or the credits—it's the shared insights and perspectives.

Another incident that Hazo remembers vividly concerned a student named Pat who one day came to class looking upset. Hazo asked if he felt all right, and the young man said, "My mother died this morning." Hazo advised him to go home immediately to be with his father, and the student did so, but Hazo was not entirely shocked that the student came to class that day. "In times like that," Hazo said, "sometimes we just don't know what to do—we feel completely lost and untethered, so we do what is familiar to us. But that's where life and learning are intertwined."

Asked about teaching in a 1989 interview with David Sokolowski, Hazo said:

SAM HAZO TEACHING IN DUQUESNE UNIVERSITY CLASSROOM, CIRCA 1978

I can't imagine not living this kind of life. I mean, if somebody would offer me a job at a major university—Princeton, Harvard—I wouldn't go. I don't care what the salary is, I wouldn't go. If somebody offered me the presidency of a college, I wouldn't take it. It doesn't appeal to me, it doesn't attract me, it's not what I want to do. And the prestige means nothing to me. I teach in a moderately-sized Catholic university in the city of Pittsburgh. It's not renowned by name like some of the schools that may have false renown. But I look around at the graduates, which is how you judge a university, and they are in positions of major importance in this city in the arts, in pharmacy, in business, in law, and in the judiciary system. And these are people I'm proud to know ... Things that might have tempted me ten or twenty years ago would now just be an annoyance to me. (224)

Although Hazo relished all of his teaching years, his "glory years" were in the 1960s and '70s, because "that was when students really seemed to be engaged and wanted to learn for learning's sake—not just to get a degree and make money. Conversations with students—both inside and outside of the classroom were the best part of the job. Conversations have no syllabus— we talked about whatever came up. It was a different time." Hazo celebrates this communion of the minds in the poem "For My Last Class of Freshmen." In the 1960s, '70s, and '80s, Duquesne was the workingman's university—where parents who didn't have the money for Ivy League schools or more expensive private colleges sent their children. "And it was a pretty damn good working-class student body. Most of the students held jobs while they went to school, and I can honestly say that I was never disappointed with any class that I taught at Duquesne."

For My Last Class of Freshmen

There is no word for what I love in you,
but it is sure, sacred and daily as bread.
I speak by indirections of a world
divisible as loaves among ourselves
and multiplied like miracles because
we share the private tables of the mind.
We join in rites and sacraments that bind

and keep us bound like vows when we face God
or Plato over coffee, books, and smoke.
Discovering the truth we always knew,
we look in one another's eyes surprised
and reconciled to what we shall recall
five years from now reclining on a plane,
exchanging socks, surrendering to pain,

dying, or saddleblocked before a birth.
Today it is enough that we rehearse
for nothing but today and everything
abreast of us impatient to be known.
If we profess no more but nothing less,
let us be tame as eagles, mad as saints,
or casual as Job in his complaints

until we learn the liturgies that sound
their psalms this second in the minstrel blood
alive from Solomon through Charlemagne
to Huckleberry's scuttlebutt to you.
Let us dare life as lovers dare the dark
and learn less stubbornly than blinded Saul
that light comes from within or not at all.

In this poem, the love of teacher for student is sacred: "We join in rites and sacraments that bind / and keep us bound like vows when we face God / or Plato over coffee, books, and smoke." This religious union, sustained throughout the poem, culminates in a powerful allusion to Paul the Apostle, who was physically blinded by God for three days before his conversion: "Let us dare life as lovers dare the dark / and learn less stubbornly than blinded Saul/ that light comes from within or not at all." Only the inner light of wisdom can save us from spiritual darkness and ignorance.

Hazo believes that teaching made him a better poet. The daily interaction with students and colleagues as well as the reading and preparation for classes made his entire professional life a constant sharing of ideas—which is, according to Hazo, essential to human existence: "Why are we here except to share? Whether you're a chef or a poet or a teacher—if you don't share insights, wisdom, affection—why the hell are you here? Just to keep it to yourself? Who gains from that? Even you don't gain from that."

The poet explores both the ordinary nature and the extraordinary results of such sharing in the next poem:

The Horizon at Our Feet

My father said, "Your work
is never over—always
one more page."
                          This
from a traveling man whose life
was always one more mile.
I told him that.
                          "Sometimes
I hate the road," he said,
"it's made me so I'm never
happy in one place.
                          Don't
you get started."
                          I never did,
spending my days at universities,
my nights at home.
                          Not
typically the academic, not
totally at home at home,
I think of how I could have lived
and come up blank.
                          What's
better than sharing all you know
and all you don't with students
who do just the same?
                          Even
on the worst of days it justifies
the time.

Or inking out
your real future on white
paper with a fountain pen
and listening to what the writing
teaches you?
Compared to walking
on the moon or curing polio,
it seems so ordinary.
And it is.
But isn't living ordinary?
For two and fifty summers
Shakespeare lived a life
so ordinary that few scholars
deal with it.
And what of Faulkner
down in ordinary Oxford, Mississippi?
Or Dickinson, the great recluse?
Or E.B. White, the writer's
writer?
Nothing extraordinary
there, but, God! what wouldn't
we give for one more page?

As mentioned previously, Hazo began his teaching career in the mid-1950s and mostly enjoyed what he called the days of "genuine university education" in the 1960s and '70s. After that, college degrees started to become more essential in gaining entry to the increasingly white-collar American workplace, tuition started to rise, and students started to feel the pressure of securing high-paying jobs after graduation. Hazo experienced that decades-long transition firsthand, and although he understood it, he didn't like it. He watched as Duquesne joined the trend toward offering "service" courses aimed at nothing more than preparing students for particular jobs after graduation. This type of career-training mentality "is against what education stands for," Hazo insists. "You're not educated to get a job. You're educated to free your mind so you can make your own decisions. College should be about discovering what you want to do—what you really love. Four years is not a very long time to make that discovery. When a university becomes a service center, it loses everything that it should stand for. And the students are the ones who get shortchanged." For Hazo, there's a certain spiritual dimension to genuine education, too, because "God has plans for everyone." Most young people entering college don't really know what they want to do for the rest of their lives—and if they *think* they do, if they seem to have their path laid out ahead of them, they will soon realize that it's not their path.[1] The exposure, the time, the space to explore possibilities: that's what a university education should provide.

Naturally, Hazo concedes that the cost of a college education has skyrocketed over the past few decades; students have more reason now than ever before to want to secure a good job so they can pay off their student loan debt. "But what I call the bourgeois habit of mind was always there—people who think that a college education should just be about getting a better job. That's not a new argument, but a college education should be so much more than that."

Hazo describes "To a Commencement of Scoundrels" as a "fed-up poem" in which he was attempting to clarify to himself that universities are not just feel-good places. It stands as both a warning to students about the many lies that fuel present-day universities and a plea for young people to pursue individuality and independent thought.

---

1. As Joseph Campbell states, "If you can see your path laid out ahead of you step by step, then you know it's not your path" (epigraph to "The Holy Surprise of Right Now").

To a Commencement of Scoundrels

My boys, we lied to you.
The world by definition stinks
of Cain, no matter what
your teachers told you. Heroes
and the fools of God may rise
like accidental green
on gray saharas, but the sand
stays smotheringly near.

Deny me if you can. Already
you are turning into personnel,
manpower, figures on a list
of earners, voters, prayers,
soldiers, payers, sums
of population tamed with forms:
last name, middle name, first name—
telephone—date of birth—

home address—age—hobbies—
experience. Tell them the truth.
Your name is Legion. You
are aged a million. Tell
them that. Say you breathe
between appointments: first day,
last day. The rest is no
one's business. Boys, the time

is prime for prophecy.
Books break down their bookends.
Paintings burst their frames.
The world is more than reason's
peanut. Homer sang it real.
Goya painted it, and Shakespeare

staged it for the pelting rinds
of every groundling of the Globe.

Wake up! Tonight the lions
hunt in Kenya. They
can eat a man. Rockets
are spearing through the sky.
They can blast a man to nothing.
Rumors prowl like rebellions.
They can knife a man. No one
survives for long, my boys.

Flesh is always in season,
lusted after, gunned, grenaded,
tabulated through machines,
incinerated, beaten to applause,
anesthetized, autopsied, mourned.
The blood of Troy beats on
in Goya's painting and the truce
of Lear. Reason yourselves

to that, my buckaroos,
before you rage for God,
country, and siss-boom-bah!
You won't, of course. Your schooling
left you trained to serve
like cocksure Paul before
God's lightning smashed
him from his saddle. So—

I wish you what I wish
myself: hard questions
and the nights to answer them,
the grace of disappointment,

and the right to seem the fool
for justice. That's enough.
Cowards might ask for more.
Heroes have died for less.

Although most of the poem is clearly, as Hazo suggests, "a
fed-up poem," in the final stanza, the poet wishes for his students
what he wishes for himself: "hard questions / and the nights to
answer them." These hard questions could arguably include any
questions that cause us to contemplate or reconsider our life
decisions. Hazo suggests that one possible question is what we
should be doing to make the world better:

What more can you do to stand for things that are worth standing for,
to oppose things that should be opposed? Those are hard questions.
Take, for example, institutions, universities, the government, whatever.
I think all institutions at some point disappoint everybody. My view
is, the sooner they disappoint you, the sooner you stop idolizing institutions. The sooner that happens, the better. It makes you realize that
disappointment is as much a part of our lives as fulfillment.

And perhaps most importantly, the poet wishes for his students
"the right to seem the fool for justice." They might be laughed at,
ridiculed, or made to feel foolish if they take a stand for justice.
But if you have the guts for it, Hazo asserts, "it's a privilege to be
called a fool for justice."

FOUR

Torch of Blood

How love
makes one what life keeps two
is where we are and when.
No ports.
No bo's'ns but ourselves.
No echo but the wake we make
to show we buccaneered that sea.

"The Darker Noon"

One of the mainstays of conversation with a married couple is to inquire how they met. We are curious about how two individuals' lives crossed paths among the myriad possible encounters. Sometimes the stories are mundane, and other times we hear surprising anecdotes that reveal fortuitous opportunities that permitted them to meet. Regardless, the story of their meeting becomes part of the narrative they share about their lives and assumes a prominent place in their memory. In the telling, the story can provide insights into their personalities, the way they look at life and the period as well. In Samuel Hazo's poetry, themes of coincidence and happenstance figure prominently. It seems fitting, then, that he would meet the one and only love of his life and wife of sixty-three years through a bit of serendipity.

At a benefit for a good friend, Hazo's aunt Katherine met Mary Anne, who was serving as one of the hostesses for the event. Aunt Katherine (Kak), who was only impressed by young women whom she deemed "exceptional"—in terms of intelligence, independence, courage, unconventional ideas, and so forth—was quite taken with Mary Anne. After the event, Aunt Kak told Hazo about Mary Anne and suggested that he meet her because "she's not like the other girls you take out—dumb."

A few days later, Hazo mentioned this conversation to a friend of his, who just happened to be one of Mary Anne's coworkers and also thought that Sam and Mary Anne should meet. This mutual friend was performing in a play at Carlow College that Mary Anne said she wanted to see. He suggested a blind date for the pair to see his play together and gave Mary Anne's phone number to Hazo.

On the designated evening, Hazo arrived at Mary Anne's house thirty minutes earlier than their agreed-upon time of seven thirty. He wanted to allow himself enough time to find her house, but he found it easily and knocked on the door at seven o'clock. Mary Anne's mother and father sat with Hazo while Mary Anne was getting ready upstairs; again, coincidentally, it turned out that her parents knew Hazo's grandfather, so they had a good conversation while they waited.

The first moment that Hazo laid eyes on Mary Anne is still crystal clear in his memory: "She was dressed in a black skirt and white blouse, and she had combed her black hair perfectly in place." Although Mary Anne was polite, Hazo noted that she seemed a bit irritated at the beginning of their date. He learned much later—after they had been dating exclusively for months— that his early arrival had slightly annoyed her.

The first act of the play was in Hazo's words "corny and sentimental—bordering on unbearable." Although neither wanted to hurt their friend's feelings, they decided to leave before the second act started. Hazo was teaching at Shady Side Academy at the time, and the boys were having a dance that night, so he asked Mary Anne if she would like to go to the dance. She said she would, and they thoroughly enjoyed the rest of their evening together.

A week later, Hazo asked Mary Anne out for a second date, this time to see Marlon Brando in the film version of Shakespeare's *Julius Caesar*. Citing a previous obligation for the evening in question, Mary Anne declined the invitation. Several weeks later, however, they did arrange a second date to see the film. After the movie, they went to a restaurant for a snack. Although Mary Anne didn't know it at the time, Hazo only had enough money to buy food for her, not for himself. "Luckily, in those days, you could get coffee for fifty cents, so I had a cup of coffee." After that night, they began seeing each other regularly, and as Hazo says, "we were never separated thereafter."

Several months later, it seemed quite obvious—at least to Hazo—that they would be married. Mary Anne mentioned one evening, however, that it would be nice to be asked. Hazo bought an engagement ring and officially proposed to Mary Anne at Schenley Park.

On June 11, 1955, the two exchanged wedding vows at St. Anne's Church in Millvale. (The church has since been converted to a social hall.) Hazo does not recall exactly how many people attended their wedding celebration, held in a Brookline theater-turned-banquet-hall. But he does remember that they received a whopping total of eighty-nine dollars in cash, which they used for their Niagara Falls and Buffalo honeymoon.

"Over the years many people, primarily women, have asked me when I was sure I wanted to marry Mary Anne," Hazo says. "It seems trite for me to say this, but something in me knew from the first time I saw her. This confirms a firm belief I have that the body knows such marital certainties from the start, then waits

for the mind to catch up and reconcile itself to what the body already is certain of."

During their courtship, Hazo wondered how his living situation would be resolved if he decided to marry. He was, after all, living with Aunt Katherine, who would be all alone without him. Once again proving herself to be unlike other women, Mary Anne resolved the potential problem before it began, stating in no uncertain terms that Kak would live with them. Hazo says, "For years, I've asked myself how many women entering marriage would welcome a mother-in-law or aunt-in-law in their married lives from the start. Not that many, I'm sure. But Mary Anne had an inborn thoughtfulness and generosity of heart that I've never seen in anyone else. This translated into a way of life that was always exemplary" ("For Mary Anne, But Moreso").

Shortly after their wedding, Hazo accepted a position in the English Department at Duquesne University. Mary Anne worked

SAM AND MARY ANNE HAZO'S WEDDING, JUNE 11, 1955

as a legal secretary downtown, and Kak still required public transportation to get to work at the time. To accommodate their various commutes, the newlyweds bought their first marital home on Jackson Street in East Liberty—a location that made sense for all of them. They lived in the city until 1962, when they bought a house in the suburbs of Upper St. Clair—a home that proved so thoroughly perfect that they never left it.

The following poem—originally published in Hazo's 1972 volume *Once for the Last Bandit*, is one of the very first love poems that Hazo wrote to his beloved wife Mary Anne.

The Darker Noon

We sail asleep from midnight
 to a beach named dawn.
You stir.
 I wake.
 My only
 stars are latitudes.
 Tomorrow
 is a shore we may not reach,
 so let it wait.
 Racoons
 are floating in their hollow
 oak cocoons.
 A milkman
 boats his bottles.
 The last
 buses trundle to their docks
 across the tire-stenciled snow.
Marking the darker noon
 of the clock, the dual arrows
 fuse into a mast that tolls
 through silence to the first birds.

The seabell of a siren wakens
you.
My wife.
My mate.
Let all the klaxons clang.
These temporary sheets
are jetsam to the moon.
How love
makes one what life keeps two
is where we are and when.
No ports.
No bo's'ns but ourselves.
No echo but the wake we make
to show we buccaneered that sea.

In this beautiful metaphor for lovemaking, the lovers have sailed the night sea, throwing the unnecessary sheets overboard. The poet, awakened when his lover stirs, enjoys a sense of complete satisfaction as he contemplates the fulfillment of their physical desire. The poet considers how "love / makes one what life keeps two" as the hands of the clock fuse at midnight. In the final stanza, we see that the lovers need neither port nor boatswain nor echo—nothing but each other and the "wake we make / to show we buccaneered that sea." It is at once playful and deeply spiritual—a poem that unites the powers of nature, love, and sexual desire.

Like many newly married couples, Sam and Mary Anne hoped to start a family right away. After four years of trying to conceive, however, they were becoming discouraged. They endured a battery of tests to discover what the problem was, but the tests all indicated that there were no medical issues preventing a pregnancy. Their doctor advised them to be patient. After six additional years of trying, the doctor conceded that they would probably never have a child. This was devastating to both Sam and Mary Anne, who had always envisioned themselves as parents. The following poem poignantly captures the anguish that all hopeful couples must feel when faced with the reality that they may never have children:

For a Son Who Will Never Be Born

When poplars spire stripped and brittle sticks
toward December stars, you will not see
the first ice catch and thicken at the curbs.
Balked of their first and last parenthesis,
the years will leave you winterless and free.

You will not know the exile's day, the nights
of thunder when the night is thunderless
and cloudless as the dark before your eyes,
nor will you grudge the waves of westering light
and the blood-bright sun ascending wonderless ...

Less brave than Simeon, I speak my fear
for flesh not yet created, named or known ...
He blessed a child begotten crucified
and mocked with a prophecy all I would spare
you with these fostering, futile words, my son.

Written in blank verse and rife with images of barrenness, the poem reveals a speaker who is trying to steel himself against the painful knowledge that he will probably never have the son that he addresses in the poem. The speaker initially tries to find solace in the knowledge that his son will never have to experience the bitterness of cold and ice because he will be "winterless and free." Likewise, his son's spirit will never be shaken by the dark night of the soul, and he will never have to endure the unending march of "wonderless" dawns and dusks in a life devoid of meaning. In the final stanza, the speaker suggests that he lacks Simeon's bravery.

In the Gospel of Luke, Simeon met Mary, Joseph, and Jesus when they presented Jesus at the temple on the fortieth day after his birth. Simeon, who had been told by the Holy Spirit that he would not die until he saw the Lord Jesus Christ, held the baby Jesus and prophesied his crucifixion. By speaking his fears about the adversities that life might bring to his son, the speaker tries to find comfort in the knowledge that he is sparing his son all the pain that life brings.

As David Sokolowski argues, we must also acknowledge the parallels between the speaker's son and the Christ child:

Christ was born under "December stars," knew "the exile's day," was crucified on the cross—"the stripped and brittle sticks," and rose as "the blood-bright sun." In the poem, Christ stands as the model of submission to time. Until the final resolution, the speaker in the poem is dead to this notion of life. In wishing to deny his son the experience of time, the speaker himself rejects time by refusing to confront his situation in time by accepting the suffering and pain it brings. (127)

Despite the genuine despair expressed in this poem, Sam and Mary Anne soon had reason to celebrate. In 1966, Hazo was invited to Jamaica by the US State Department to give a series of talks on poetry. Mary Anne was suffering with a case of the flu at the time, and her doctor suggested that she accompany Sam because the tropical weather would accelerate her recovery. On their first day in Jamaica, they learned that Queen Elizabeth II and her husband Prince Philip would be arriving for a visit the following day—and as luck would have it—the royal visit wiped Hazo right off the schedule for five days. Sam and Mary Anne spent the time relaxing by the pool and enjoying a commitment-free week. "It was in effect a honeymoon," Hazo says with a roguish smile. "And it had consequences."

Back in Pittsburgh for more than a month, Mary Anne found herself feeling under the weather once again. They called the doctor, who asked for a urine specimen and promised same-day results. Later that afternoon, Hazo answered the phone in his Duquesne University office and heard the doctor utter those precious words: "Mary Anne is definitely pregnant." Wanting to give Mary Anne the news in person, Hazo walked to her office in the Koppers Building, where she worked as the executive secretary of the Allegheny County Bar Association. On his way, he purchased the entire five-volume set of childrearing books by Dr. Spock. Hazo reminisces:

She was alone in the office when I arrived, and she looked startled when she saw me.

"Anything wrong?" she asked.

"You better keep the middle of November open."

"Why?"

"You're going to have a baby."

Her expression changed from mild surprise to disbelief, and then she started to cry. (Later she told me that she thought I was kidding because the day just happened to be April Fool's Day.) Finally, she looked at me and, smiling through her tears, she said "I'll bet this is the first time that a husband ever told his wife that she was going to have a baby!"

Since Mary Anne was approaching forty when she finally became pregnant, hers was considered a high-risk pregnancy, and she was monitored carefully by her doctor. But despite the risks, Mary Anne knew she and her baby would be just fine because, Hazo says, "She felt better during her pregnancy than she did at any time in her entire life." Her pregnancy was easy and problem-free from start to finish, and their son was born perfectly healthy and happy.

When Hazo talks about November 15, 1966—the day of his son's birth—he immediately recalls three significant coincidences that have woven a place for themselves in the fabric of that time. The first concerned Aunt Katherine. Although she lived with them, Kak sent Sam and Mary Anne a Christmas card in December 1964—something she had never done before. In the card, she wrote, "I hope you have a boy next year." And here they were, just two years after Kak's hopeful prophecy, welcoming their precious son into the world. The second coincidence was that Hazo's cousin's wife Nancy just happened to be one of the nurses on the maternity ward that day—and she was the first to hold the infant Sam. And finally, the Duquesne University Sigma Lambda sorority members (for whom Mary Anne served as advisor) were visiting St. Clair Hospital as a service project on the day Hazo's son was born. When the proud father went to the nursery to see his baby for the first time, the young women were all packed around the nursery window making a considerable fuss over their advisor's new baby. Hazo shakes his head and smiles as he enjoys the memory: "I couldn't see my son at all, but the girls assured me that he was beautiful!"

Once the sorority sisters cleared a path for the proud father, Hazo was struck by another visual that he will never forget. The nurses had placed his son's bassinette next to a newborn baby girl with a gorgeous complexion, black hair, and beautiful blue eyes. And there was Hazo's son beside her—with olive skin and a full head of hair that the nurses had combed flawlessly. "He looked like a senator," Hazo recalls with a chuckle. "And the two of them looked like a young married couple!"

During the pregnancy, Mary Anne asked Sam to develop a list of potential baby names he liked. Although he had done so, Mary Anne dismissed the list after the baby was born and said simply, "His name is Samuel Robert, after you and your brother." This was an extremely thoughtful gesture, according to Hazo, since Robert was not married. "Mary Anne wanted to perpetuate his name along with mine—another example of the kind of inborn thoughtfulness that was typical of her."

Naturally, Hazo's students at Duquesne were eager to hear about their professor's new baby. Back in the classroom the day

SAM ROBERT

after his son's birth (this was 1966—long before paternity leave existed in America), Hazo told his students about his baby, mentioning, of course, that his name was Samuel Robert. He admits that there may have been "a tinge of fatherly pride" in his voice when he reported the name. One of his female students, who was from Ecuador, said, "You remind me so much of my father. My mother had my two sisters and me before my brother was born. My father used to tell my mother, 'If it's a boy, I don't want him to be named Valentin. That's my name, and it was my father's name, and it was his father's name, and none of us had luck with this name.' When my brother was born, my father came home from the hospital. He was smiling and smoking a cigar. My sister and I asked, 'Papa, what's his name?' He puffed his cigar and said 'Valentin.'"

There was never a happier moment in their lives, Hazo avers, than when this "miraculous baby" was born. "Love creates moments that transcend time. When our son was born, that was like a gift to us from God" (qtd. in Sokolowski, 255).

When it was time for Samuel Robert's baptism, Mary Anne suggested that they ask Aunt Anna to be their son's godmother. Hazo's aunt Anna loved children; she had three children of her own but no grandchildren and no godchildren. She was seventy

SAM ROBERT WITH AUNT ANNA

years old when they asked her to be Sam Robert's godmother, and it changed her world.

Hazo said of Aunt Anna:

If ever a person was destined to be a godmother, it was Aunt Anna. She actually worked in a store specializing in children's clothing, and the children of her customers loved her. In fact, everyone—not only children—loved her. Some people suggested that Aunt Anna might be too old to be a godmother, but age meant nothing to Mary Anne. She ignored all the suggestions and, in choosing, created one of the most beautiful and devotional relationships I have ever seen. Our son was always totally happy when he was with Aunt Anna. They talked, played games and laughed together. She even let him cut her hair. They could never be together long enough. Time after time they were complete-ly happy just sitting side by side and saying nothing at all for hours. That was a special norm for all of our son's childhood years. Remarkable. ("For Mary Anne, ButMoreso")

The value of silence arises in several of Hazo's poems, particularly in contemplations of love, gratitude, and pain. In remembering Sam Robert's relationship with his godmother, Hazo explains how this idea of "articulate silence" operated: "Talk is compensa-tion for the lack of perfection. The more perfect the contact with some person, some thing, the more you move beyond language… The more perfect the relationship, the less the need to fill the void. Silence is very eloquent that way. You talk with the eyes" (qtd. in Furlong, 40).

Aunt Anna was Sam Robert's go-to person for a wide vari-ety of eventualities. With a chuckle, Hazo remembers his son's response any time he thought he might be in trouble with his parents: "Please take me to Aunt Anna's house." Despite the fact that they never once granted his request, Sam Robert consis-tently made the appeal. Aunt Anna lived to be eighty-nine and was Sam's perfect godmother for nineteen years. Hazo celebrates their priceless bond in the following poem:

A Love Like No Other

It happens rarely, if at all.
Age means little.
History
means less.
All that matters
is the mystery.
From infancy
to manhood our son's love
for his godmother never lessened.

Sixty years between them
made no difference.
                    For hours
they could sit in the same room,
say little or nothing and be
perfectly happy.
                    Once
she even let him cut
her hair ...
                    A decade later
she told my wife during
their last moments together,
"A very nice young man
always comes to see me,
and he looks just like your son."

Samuel Robert was showered with love from every possible angle, and according to his father, "never presented us with a single problem that I can remember." Hazo wrote "Carol of a Father," his first published poem extolling fatherhood, in 1972.

Carol of a Father

He runs ahead to ford a flood of leaves—
he suddenly a forager and I
the lagging child content to stay behind
and watch the gold upheavals at the curb
submerge his surging ankles and subside.

A word could leash him back or make him turn
and ask me with his eyes if he should stop.
One word, and he would be a son again
and I a father sentenced to correct
a boy's caprice to shuffle in the drifts.

Ignoring fatherhood, I look away
and let him roam in his Octobering
to mint the memory of those few falls
when a boy can wade the quiet avenues
alone, and the sound of leaves solves everything.

The intimacy of the father-son bond served as the inspiration for this poem. If the relationship of God and Christ is the relationship of Father and Son, Hazo posits, then every father and son is a reflection of God and Christ. It's an ongoing life that the father is responsible for, and the very nature of it is spiritual. The depth and significance of this connection—unabashedly religious in nature—are clear in "Torch of Blood":

Torch of Blood

Down on my knees and palms
        beside my son, I rediscover
        doormats, rugnaps,
        rockerbows and walljoints
        looming into stratospheres
        of ceiling.
                        A telephone
        rings us apart.
                        I'm plucked
        by God's hooks up
        from Scylla through an open door,
        Charybdis in a socket and a Cyclops
        lamp that glares floorlevel
        souls away from too much
        light to lesser darknesses.
What god in what machine
        shall pluck my son?

               Amid
the Carthage of toys, he waits
unplucked, unpluckable.
                        I
gulliver my way around
his hands and leave him stalled
before the Matterhorn of one
of seven stairs.
                  Floorbound,
he follows, finds and binds
my knees with tendrils of receiver
cord.
            I'm suddenly Laocoon
at bay, condemned to hear
some telephoning Trojan offer
me a more prudential life
where I can wake insured
against disaster, sickness, age
and sundry acts of Genghis
God.
            Meanwhile, I'm slipping
tentacles and watching my
confounding namesake toddle free....
Bloodbeats apart, he shares
with me the uninsurable air.
We breathe it into odysseys
where everyone has worlds to cross
and anything can happen.
Like some blind prophet
cursed with truth, I wish
my son his round of stumbles
to define his rise.

                                Nothing
          but opposites can ground him
          to the lowest heights where men
          go, Lilliputian but redeemable.
     Before or after Abraham,
          what is the resurrection and the life
          except a father's word
          remembered in his son?
                                What more
          Is Isaac or the Lord?
                           Breath
          and breathgiver are one, and both
          are always now as long
          as flesh remembers.
                                No
          testament but that lives on.
     The torch of blood is anyone's
          to carry.
                    I say so as my son's
          father, my father's son.

Sam, Mary Anne, and Sam Robert were an inseparable trio, spending every moment of free time together. Although she enjoyed her work as the executive secretary of the Allegheny County Bar Association and was even honored as one of the three top legal secretaries in the United States, Mary Anne resigned her position to be at home with their son. She did, however, accept a position working from home as a travel consultant for individuals and group tours. This was the perfect job for Mary Anne because it allowed her occasional travel with the groups she consulted for—and she loved to travel. Unlike Hazo, who has always felt rather displaced by travel, "The world was Mary Anne's book," Hazo says, and she wanted to read it all.

SAM HAZO WITH HIS SON, SAM ROBERT

SAM HAZO WITH HIS SON, SAM ROBERT

When a speaking engagement or lecture would draw Hazo away from home for a night or more, he knew that Mary Anne and Sam would go about their daily activities and be just fine without him. This was not necessarily the case, however, on the occasions that father and son found themselves alone in the house without mom. Hazo tells a priceless story about the time Mary Anne traveled to Venice for a week and a half with one of the group tours she had arranged, leaving "the men" to their own devices at home. "We were bumping into one another in this house," Hazo says, "and we didn't know what to do with ourselves, so I suggested that we call Mary Anne." Sam Robert was just a little boy—maybe six or seven years old at the time.

SAM, MARY ANNE, AND SAM ROBERT HAZO

Worried by the unplanned phone call, Mary Anne immediately asked if something was wrong. After assuring her that nothing was wrong and talking for a while, Hazo asked his son if he wanted to speak with his mother. To his father's surprise, Sam Robert shook his head "no," so his dad tried to convince him: "Come on, Sam, it's long distance—talk to your mom." But Sam Robert held his ground: "No, I will write her a letter." And write a letter he did—which didn't arrive at the hotel until after Mary Anne had left. It was delivered to their house two weeks after Mary Anne's return home. Hazo vividly recalls the letter, which Mary Anne kept as one of her treasures:

Dear Mom,

I loved you before you went, I love you while you're away, and I'll love you when you come back. I have a little cold but I think I'm getting better. Dad and I almost nearly can't get along without you.

Love,

Sam

Although surviving without the uncontested commander of household affairs for eleven days produced an amusing memory that both parents cherished, father and son did not share similar feelings about the absence. Whereas Sam Robert preferred to convey his feelings in writing—and include just enough mention of a "little cold" to keep her concerned—his father wanted nothing more desperately than to hear his wife's beautiful voice. That need to connect with her across the continents inspired the following poem, originally published in *To Paris* (1981):

Long Distance Isn't

Separated by a sea, two shores,
    the clans of Vercingetorix, the Brenner
    Pass, the boot of Italy
    from just below the knee to halfway
    down the calf, we nix them all
    by phone.
                Our voices kiss.
Who cares if the Atlantic bashes
    Maine, Land's End, or Normandy?
We leapfrog hemispheres the way
    the mind cavorts through God-knows-what
    millennia, what dynasties, what
    samples of our kind from
    australopithecus to Charlie Chaplin.

The body's place?
                    Cross latitude
     by longitude, and it is there.
The body's age?
               Count up
     from birth or back from death,
     and it is there.
                         But words?
We launch them out like vows
     against the wind.
                         Creating what we are,
     they wing through seas and continents
     and make us more than elegies
     to yesterday.
                    Forget the cost.
Talk louder and ignore the static.
Pretend we're walking through the dark.
Don't stop.
               Don't stop or look
     behind you.
                    As long as you
     keep talking, I can find you.

Hazo has always been fascinated by the way innocent children view the world—when their curiosity prompts them to ask
endless questions every day, and their imagination allows them
to dream the most wonderfully impossible things. With an eye
toward capturing that sense of wonder and possibility while Sam
Robert still possessed it, his father wrote the following poem:

The Duel That Is Vertical

Nearing the world of nine
     Novembers, he astounds you,

makes you dream of reruns,
maddens you for missing what
can only happen once or never.
Cheek against your arm, he asks
    you how we hear—exactly how?
You talk of waves, vibrations,
    tympany and then give up.
Lately you give up on more
    and more—on God, on death,
    on whether goldfish sleep
    or where the sky stops.
                        Before
    undoubtful doubts, you stand
    on ignorance.
                    You stall the vaccination
    of the facts
            You answer mystery
    with mystery.
                    Headed as a pair
    for sleep, you play a game
    that knights you in the name
    of wonder.
                    Flying buses
    stand for jets—freighters
    are sea-trucks—applause is happy
    noise, and so on.
                    He leads
You counter.
                Almost asleep,
    he tells you how he dreams
    of chasing lions through Alaska
    on his bike.

> You ask him
> if he's heard there are
> no lions in Alaska.
> He says
> there are if he can dream there are.
> Before undreamers undeceive him,
> you believe him, dream by dream.

The "duel" at issue in this delightful poem is between two different ways of seeing the world—the adult's way that has been vaccinated by facts, and the child's way—full of wonder and possibility and dreams. The poem begins with the child asking the speaker questions about how we hear, whether fish sleep, and where the sky stops. After feeble attempts to explain, the speaker gives up and chooses instead to "answer mystery / with mystery" and allow the child to take the lead in their imagination game. By the end of the poem, the roles of the child and speaker have completely reversed: the poet is now asking the questions, and the child is offering the answers. Seeing beauty in the child's pure sense of wonder and wanting to preserve that moment of innocence, the speaker elects to "believe him, dream by dream."

Sam and Mary Anne relished every moment of Sam Robert's childhood, but Hazo insists that Mary Anne was the more perceptive parent, commending her for recognizing and encouraging their son's love for music at a young age. As a toddler, he watched *The Little Drummer Boy* on television. Hazo recalls that young Sam immediately began to drum with both hands on all available household surfaces—furniture, cushions, countertops—so Mary Anne bought him a drum for Christmas. "On the next Christmas she bought him another drum," Hazo says. "On the following Christmas, she gave him a set of drums. When he was four, he began taking drum lessons."

By the time Sam Robert entered high school, he had developed into a very good drummer. But during young Sam's formative years, his father was also sharing his own love for baseball. Hazo writes in his journal that he's glad he instilled in his son a love for what he calls "bankable treasures" such as poetry, books, words, music, and sport. A game that is deeply engrained in American culture, baseball is "mysteriously shareable, particularly between sons and their fathers." In addition to many regular-season games, Hazo took his son to one divisional play-off game (when the Pirates beat the Reds) and a World Series game when the Pirates outplayed the Orioles. According to Hazo, baseball provides key moments and memories that fathers and sons will cherish forever. He and his son both remember when the pitcher for the Red Sox inexplicably lost his nerve against the Mets. "You could see it in his face," Hazo recalls, and the Mets went on to win the series. "Moments like these," Hazo says, "go beyond mere sports and leave a legacy that people can talk about for years afterwards."

Young Sam played on a community baseball team during high school. But after breaking his leg on a slide into home base, he was sidelined for a year. While other kids might have moped on the bench feeling sorry for themselves, Sam Robert immediately shifted his focus to his other love: music. He joined a band, and from that moment on, he has never looked back. He attended Duquesne University to study music and subsequently became a music teacher, a conductor, and ultimately a world-renowned composer.

Hazo believes there's a spiritual dimension to his son's journey—that God has plans for each of us. One of his most famous poems, "The Holy Surprise of Right Now," begins with an epigraph by Joseph Campbell: "If you can see your path laid out ahead of you step by step, then you know it's not your path."

"That's called life," Hazo says. "And life imposes its own choices on you. If you choose what you don't love, you can fail; you might survive; you can't excel. If you choose what you love, you can't fail; you will survive; and you can excel. Excellence is impossible in any other circumstance." This philosophy grounds Hazo's belief that college students should choose majors based on what they love doing instead of what they think will lead to high-paying jobs. "If you're doing something just for a paycheck, you can come to hate the work and hate yourself for doing it. But when you love something, the sky's the limit." He returns to the spiritual dimension: "Trust in God that it will lead to something."

When Hazo talks about his son, he does so with a mixture of pride, admiration, appreciation, and deeply abiding love. He says, "Once you're a father, you're a father forever. It's non-transferable. And it fulfills you as a man. Here I was through thirty-eight years as a son, a brother, an uncle, a teacher, a former student, a military officer, a cousin—everything but a father." And once he became a father, he remarks, he has never been the same since. "Sam brought a new life to his mother and me, and I wouldn't change a minute of it."

Shortly after graduating from Duquesne University, Samuel Robert met Dawn, the woman who would become his wife and the mother of their three children—Sam, Anna, and Sarah. Hazo wrote this poem to honor their marriage:

Once Upon a Wedding

For Sam and Dawn

Watching two lives converge
    through all your predecessors down
    the centuries to you is miracle
    enough.
        But all that is
is history.
           You're more than that.
If choosing is the most that freedom
    means, you're free.

If choosing
one you love for life
is freedom at its best,
you're at your best today.
No wonder we're exuberant.
Today's become an instant
anniversary for all of us.
You've brought us back to what's
the most important choice
of all.
You've shown that where
we come from matters less
than who we are, and who
we are is what we choose
to be . . .
We're all familiar
with the risks.
No matter how
or whom we love, we know
we're each on loan to one
another for a time.
We know
we're God's employees picked
for unforeseen assignments
we'll be given on the way.
The secret
is to love until the summoning,
regardless of the odds . . .
Go now
together in the unison of mates.
Go happily with all our hopes
and all our blessings.
And with God's.

According to Hazo, Dawn has made their lives even richer than they were previously, keeping them all "in love together and intact" ("In Troth"). To honor their twentieth wedding anniversary, Hazo wrote "Twenty and Not Counting"—a poem celebrating the beautiful family they have created and the deep love they share:

From Twenty and Not Counting

Today for you the sum
    of one plus one still stays
    at one plus Sam, Anna and Sarah.
You love each other near,
    and yet the times when you're
    together seem to pass
    so quickly even when you make
    the time.
        You want those moments
    never to be over.
            That's all
that matters now.
            Or ever.

Hazo becomes unabashedly emotional when he discusses his relationship with his son. To this day, Sam Robert is a "regular guy and a true friend." Hazo explains that out of all the men he has ever met, he doesn't know anybody who can touch his son. Wholly dedicated to his family and without an ounce of hypocrisy in him, Sam Robert is "a good dad, a good husband, and a good son. He's a real man in the best sense of the word ... I love [him] so much that at times it reduces me to tears" (Journal). Hazo's total commitment to his adult son radiates from the lines of the following poem, with the bond they share over baseball serving as emblem for a love that grows ever deeper and richer as time passes.

SAM ROBERT AND DAWN'S WEDDING, DECEMBER 16, 1995

Father and Son

1

I must be shrinking.

He seems
much taller than he was
a year ago.

And wiser.
He has his mother's kindness
and the gift of spotting fakery
at sight.

He works at what
he loves where clocks have no
credentials.

His music lasts
like love, and those who play it
tell him that.

Though
family means most, completing
what needs doing ranks first
with him.

That's why I love him
as the son-husband-father
who's exceeded every hope
I dared to have.

He's all
I wanted most but more
than I deserve.

Though two
we're one enough to know what's
dearer than love of friend
for friend or brother for brother.
That's ours now and always.

2

We pitched and caught with mitts
    we never could dispose of—
    their weathered leather supple
    after thirty years, their pockets
    shaped by pitches gloved
    as strikes, their webbings frayed,
    their colors curing into faded
    tans obscured with dirt
    that scuffed their trademarks
    to a smudge but still left readable
    the names of Campanella and the great
    DiMaggio before each man
    was chosen for the Hall of Fame,
    then claimed in turn by paraplegia
    and infarction after Brooklyn opted
    for Los Angeles while Stengel's Yankees
    kept their pinstripes in the Bronx,
    and we survived to treasure
    two outdated mitts now good
    for nothing but nostalgia every time
    we flex our fingers in them
    to be sure the past still fits.

FIVE

In Troth

Who says that those who've gone
are ever out of sight or mind?
They're present but invisible.

They visit

when they choose.

They rule the world.

"Alone with Presences"

When the subject of love and loss is broached in conversation, prose, or poetry, a line from Alfred Lord Tennyson's epic poem *In Memoriam A.H.H.* usually comes to mind: "Tis better to have loved and lost, / Than never to have loved at all." Depending on our life experiences, we can grasp on some level the devastating emptiness after the loss of one we truly love that Tennyson describes. Sam Hazo has an intimate understanding of the sadness Tennyson expresses. Following the loss of his beloved soulmate, Mary Anne, in 2016, Hazo has written a number of poems and an unforgettable essay, "For Mary Anne, But Moreso," that describe his innermost feelings as he opens his heart to the desolation he suffers and, like Tennyson, emerges with gratitude for the precious gift of the love they shared.

For sixty-three years, Sam and Mary Anne shared everything—good, bad, and indifferent—because "that's what marriage is." They could talk about anything, and although they did not agree on everything, they agreed on the basics. Mary Anne, for example, was not too keen on poetry (including Shakespeare) unless it moved her. They did, however, have the same heroes and think the same men fools—the litmus test for true friendship, according to American poet Mark Van Doren. The one thing they always had in common was how they felt about each other. One of the qualities that Hazo admired and appreciated most about Mary Anne was her "inborn thoughtfulness and generosity of heart [which] translated into a way of life that was always exemplary" ("For Mary Anne, But Moreso"). Possessed of many of both his mother's and Aunt Katherine's finest qualities, Mary Anne was capable of a deep and steady love. "And she had the courage to back it up," Hazo says. Writing in his journal years before her death, Hazo describes Mary Anne's inherent goodness: "[Mary Anne] truly cares about people. She'll go out of her way for someone in need and never feel that she's going out of her way." Although he could easily point to numerous illustrations of her generous spirit, Hazo highlights the following three stories, which he believes capture her essence:

On one occasion a close friend of hers was anxious to buy a stereo set for her two daughters for Christmas but simply could not afford it. At that time Mary Anne had accumulated numerous books filled with what were then called Green Stamps. If you purchased merchandise at a particular franchise, you earned Green Stamps that you pasted on a book for that purpose. The stamps were the equivalent of money and could be redeemed for products. Mary Anne checked and found that she had enough Green Stamps that could be exchanged for a complete stereo. Without a second thought, she gave the books to her friend and never mentioned a word of this to anyone even though she had been collecting the stamps for more than four years.

On another occasion her niece Mary Romah was expecting her first child and had gone into labor after driving herself to Mercy Hospital. Her mother had promised to travel from Detroit to be with her but was taken ill and could not come. Her husband, to whom she had been introduced by Mary Anne, was a commercial airline pilot and was in flight at the time. Mary Anne somehow learned of this, drove to the hospital at 1:00 in the morning and stayed with Mary for what turned out to be a twelve-hour labor. From that time her niece has referred to Mary Anne as her "mother."

On still another occasion we visited the University of Notre Dame on the occasion of the reunion of my class of 1949. During the visit, there was a luncheon, and Mary Anne, for whom Notre Dame was first, last and always, found herself seated beside the new President, Father John Jenkins. The two of them were very much at home in one another's company, and Mary Anne spoke highly and endearingly of him thereafter. Some years later I received a letter from Father Jenkins in which he offered me an honorary doctorate. The degree is sacred to me, and I am convinced to this day that Mary Anne had something to do with my receiving it even though she acted as surprised as I was when Father Jenkins' letter told me that I was chosen to receive it. ("For Mary Anne, But Moreso")

Hazo also credits Mary Anne with one of his truly distinguishing poetic hallmarks—the ability to recite his poems from memory. Poetry enthusiasts know well that even the most seasoned poets "read" their poems at poetry events; it is fully anticipated and accepted behavior in the poetry community. But early on, Hazo explains, Mary Anne was attending one of his readings. When he got up to read, Mary Anne asked why he was taking the book to the podium with him. "You wrote them," she pointed out. "Don't you know them?" This simple question was the catalyst that ultimately changed Hazo's recitation methods, making him one of a rare breed of contemporary poets who recite their poems to audiences instead of reading them. Mary Anne's query made him think back to his participation on the debate team at

Notre Dame. He remembered that when he took notecards to the podium with him, he looked at them too much and began to rely on them. But when he started leaving the cards behind and debating without them, it jumpstarted his brain: "Your mind does things for you that you never thought it could do," Hazo explains. "People think they can't do something until they're in a position where they have no option. Then they find out that they can do it. Mind and memory work that way."

After more than fifty years of memorized recitations, Hazo says he is no longer nervous about being at the podium sans book. He admits, however, that he is always apprehensive about potentially missing a word or a line. Fortunately, when he has on occasion forgotten a word, another word has come to him in the instant. And sometimes he changes words purposefully because the original printed word is not as effective as what he comes up with later. As is the case with all great presentations, it comes down to practice. Hazo thoroughly reviews and practices the poems he will "say" before an event in the same way a seasoned stage actor will have to review and clean up the lines when a couple of years have passed between performances. "Like a donkey, you can overload your memory," Hazo says. "So when you feel that it's overloaded, you need to dump whatever you can't carry." After that, everything that you can't forget no matter how hard you try—well, Hazo says, that's "all that's worth remembering." Hazo's poem "Understory" eloquently explains this philosophy:

Understory

It's not that sometimes I forget.
I'm told that everybody does.
What troubles me is how
whatever I've forgotten trebles
in importance the more I keep
forgetting it.

Some word . . .

Some place . . .

Today a student from the Class
of Way Back When
seemed certain I'd remember him
by name.

I tried and tried
before I had to ask . . .

Though students
and ex-students are my life,
I must admit that I remember
most of the best, all
of the worst, many who have left
this world and not that many
of the rest.

It leaves me wondering . . .

Is memory a beast that sheds
its baggage as it goes?
Are facts by definition destined
for oblivion?

Or is it absolute
that what I can't forget no matter
how I try is all that's worth
remembering?

I know a mother
of four sons who mixes up
their names.

Ollie is Bennett.

Bennett is Drew.

Drew

is Christopher.

> Facing one,
> she'll travel down the list before
> she'll ask, "Tell me your name,
> dear boy."
> Outsiders realize
> they're all one boy to her,
> regardless of their names.
> She knows
> them by their souls.
> That reassures me.

For JoAnn Bevilacqua-Weiss

Hazo feels deep appreciation for many benefits that resulted from being Mary Anne's partner for sixty-three years. Among the most life-altering benefits was her role in the creation of the International Poetry Forum (IPF), which he attributes to her intuitive understanding and responses to people and social situations. In his essay "To Mary Anne, But Moreso," Hazo explains how Mary Anne's commonsense advice completely redirected the trajectory of his career:

On one occasion, I had invited the poet W. H. Auden to speak at Duquesne. Introducing him, I said that it was unfortunate that there were not forums in major American cities where poets could speak to the public at large and not only to students and teachers. There was a man in the audience named Theodore Hazlett, who was the Director of the A. W. Mellon Educational and Charitable Trust. He called me the day after Auden's appearance and invited me to lunch. During the luncheon, he told me that he was orienting the Trust toward the arts and found my suggestion of having a civic forum for poets in Pittsburgh and elsewhere interesting and thought it feasible to start such a forum in the city if I were willing to direct it. I was stunned. Mr. Hazlett told me to think it over and contact him with my decision.

While we were having dinner that evening, I told Mary Anne about the luncheon and asked her if she knew Mr. Hazlett. Since he was also a lawyer, she did know of him and said he had a good reputation in the city. I then explained his offer to me and said I didn't know if it was a "martini" idea or not. Mary Anne then added, "What do you have to lose by taking him seriously?" I took her advice, and within a year the International Poetry Forum was born, and I directed it for forty-three years. More than eight hundred poets, actors and performers, i.e., Archibald MacLeish, Richard Wilbur, Linda Pastan, Gregory Peck, Princess Grace of Monaco, Eva Marie Saint, Victoria de los Angeles, James Earl Jones, Stanley Kunitz, Yevgeny Yevtushenko and others, presented poetry programs in Pittsburgh during that era and created a legacy for poetry that is as significant as any anywhere, including the Library of Congress. Again, I owe the Forum's origin to Mary Anne's prudent but salient advice.

The founding of the International Poetry Forum significantly altered Hazo's professional concerns. Although he continued to teach at Duquesne University and write prolifically during the years that the IPF flourished (1966–2009), Hazo invested a great deal of time and energy in directing the forum. Funded through a grant from Theodore L. Hazlett, director of the A. W. Mellon Educational and Charitable Trust, the goal of the forum was to create a space where "poetry could speak for itself in a public setting" (*Poets Reciting Their Own Poetry*). In *The Autobiographers of Everybody: A Mosaic Portrait of the International Poetry Forum* (2011), Hazo explains that he was interested in establishing "something with centrifugal force—something that would radiate its energy outward from its core. Hence, the idea of a forum, a place where poets and actors—like citizens who came to the agora in ancient Athens—could be invited to recite poems in front of people who voluntarily came and paid to hear them. Each recital, of course, would be one of a kind" (1). And for forty-three years, the International Poetry Forum did just that—offering poets and performers from all over the world a place to share their art, and providing poetry enthusiasts a place to nourish their souls—right in the heart of Pittsburgh, Pennsylvania.

Archibald MacLeish accepted Hazo's invitation to be the IPF's inaugural poet on October 19, 1966. In his opening, he made the following remark about poetry:

The most important thing about this evening is the evening itself. A festival devoted to poetry over a period of time may or may not do anything for the city in which it is established, but it can't help making a difference to poetry. And poetry is important. For poetry—using that word in its universal sense to include all the arts, the whole labor of the arts, is the sole means we have of learning the answer to the essential question—the question of who we are ... And the need to know who we are has never in human history been greater... We have somehow lost contact with ourselves, lost touch with ourselves, we don't know who we are. We know what we can do but not why and to what end. And there is only one salvation from this situation, and that is the rediscovery of who we are and what we are as human beings—the rediscovery of our human selves—and this, only the arts are capable of doing. These are the instruments by which over a great period of time, men have put down their discoveries of themselves. It's all in Sappho, that incredible fragment of Sappho: "The moon is down / and the Pleiades are gone, / it is the middle of the night and time passes, / time passes, and I lie alone." It's been all through literature, all through the arts, all through poetry, from the beginning, little by little, piece by piece—the discovery of who we are. We go on teaching poetry, teaching literature, as though it were some kind of a prerequisite to being a cultivated human being, but poetry is the absolutely essential food of living a human life. It is for this reason that I don't begin by saying that I'm proud to be here or happy to be here. I feel much more deeply than that. I feel that this is a very important moment in my life ... and in your lives. (International Poetry Forum Digital Archive)

In fact, the International Poetry Forum proved to be a priceless gift to the city of Pittsburgh as well as a boon to the world of poetry. No other venue like it existed—this was the first and only initiative of its kind in Pittsburgh.

The IPF attracted world-class poets and performers from the United States and thirty-eight other countries to its stage. Notable Nobel Prize awardees included Saul Bellow, Seamus Heaney, Czeslaw Milosz, Octavio Paz, and Derek Walcott; Pulitzer Prize-winning poets and writers included Galway Kinnell, Maxine Kumin, W. S. Merwin, Robert Penn Warren, and Richard Wilbur. Playwright heavyweights Edward Albee and Tennessee Williams, and renowned novelists Chinua Achebe and Kurt Vonnegut also graced the forum stage, as did distinguished public figures such as Queen Noor of Jordan, Princess Grace of Monaco, and Senator Eugene McCarthy. Many of the world's most highly respected actors and actresses also performed at the International Poetry Forum, including Academy Award recipients Jose Ferrer, Anthony Hopkins, Gregory Peck, and Sir Peter Ustinov; Emmy awardee Maureen Stapleton; and Tony Award winner Jessica Tandy. Acclaimed vocalists, musicians, and composers such as Ruby Dee, Vivica Genaux, Dame Cleo Laine, and Gian Carlo Menotti proved to be huge crowd-pleasers at the International Poetry Forum— often sharing the stage with promising new poets who were just starting to make a name for themselves.

Asked why he invited musicians, singers, and actors to perform with the poets, Hazo explains that poetry includes anything that actuates the imagination, from complex art forms such as dance and acting performed on the world stage to simple acts of nature observed from a kitchen window: "I can watch the deer walk in the backyard and to me that's a poetic moment because they know how to do it."

Hundreds of devoted season ticket holders as well as students, teachers, and fans of individual poets and performers

SAM HAZO AT THE INTERNATIONAL POETRY FORUM IN PITTSBURGH

PRINCESS GRACE OF MONACO PRESENTS "BIRDS, BEASTS, AND FLOWERS"
FOR THE INTERNATIONAL POETRY FORUM, 1978

INTERNATIONAL POETRY FORUM AUDIENCE IN CARNEGIE MUSIC HALL, PITTSBURGH

comprised the IPF audiences each month. After just a few years, the celebration of poetry had become a mainstay of Pittsburgh's cultural life.

Ultimately extending far beyond its original purpose, the International Poetry Forum developed and sponsored the Poets in the Schools Program, copresented poetry programs at Washington DC's Smithsonian Institution, and funded the publication of many books by award-winning poets (in conjunction with the University of Pittsburgh Press).

While it flourished for forty-three years, the International Poetry Forum was unable to survive the failing economy of 2009, and it closed its doors that year. But thanks to Sam Hazo's devotion to sharing the spoken word, thousands of people learned what he always knew: "The heard poem mints a memory that lasts within us like a song. All we have to do is listen to make it ours" (*Actors and Actresses Reciting Poems*).

Six years after the closing of the International Poetry Forum, Hazo wrote an article that related a few of the more memorable stories, moments, and quips from his years as director. Published in the *Pittsburgh Post-Gazette*, the article included the following wonderfully entertaining anecdotes, most of which occurred during interactions Hazo had with the headliners before and after the readings:

Polish writer Jerzy Kosinski, who agreed to be the master of ceremonies for the Forum's 20th anniversary program in 1986, told me without emotion about an experience he had in 1969. He was living in Paris and received an invitation to attend a party in Los Angeles. He agreed to attend and booked his flight. At the airport, he was asked by a boarding official for his final destination. Kosinski said it would be Paris because he planned to return immediately after the party. The official responded that he was already in Paris and told him to step out of line. After much altercation that led nowhere ("It was too much for the French mind," he said), Kosinski missed his flight and the party. This was the party at

Roman Polanski's home at which Charles Manson's coterie murdered Polanski's wife, Sharon Tate, and four others[1] ...

I invited Alexander Scourby to present an evening of contemporary Greek poetry. Scourby, of Greek lineage and a narrator of multiple radio, television and film features, also recorded numerous audio books. I noticed that there were many young blind people in the audience. After the program ended, the blind students came backstage to meet Scourby and touch his hand. When I asked why, they said, "Because he is our book."

In the late 1960s and the 1970s, Yevgeny Yevtushenko and Andrei Voznesensky were Russia's prime literary exports. Both were excellent reciters of their poetry from memory. It was the Forum's invitation to Yevtushenko through the State Department that made his first visit to the United States possible, and a crowd packed the Carnegie Music Hall to hear him. As he made a few preliminary remarks, someone shouted from the balcony that he should stand closer to the microphone because he could not be heard. After a pause, Yevtushenko said in English, "You come closer to me." And the audience did, and the evening was unforgettable....

When John Updike read his poems here, his parents traveled from eastern Pennsylvania to hear him. Upright, reserved and modest, Mr. and Mrs. Wesley Updike looked like they had stepped out of a Grant Woods painting. When I said they should be quite proud of their son, Wesley Updike responded, "We do hope he makes a contribution." ...

When Brooke Shields appeared in the Forum's "Turn of the Century Impromptu" with James Earl Jones and David Conrad, many assumed that her fame and beauty precipitated the invitation. What they did not know was that she knew French literature, spoke French fluently and had a degree from Princeton with French as her forté. I asked her to begin her portion of the program by reading without preliminary remarks a poem by Jacques Prevert. As soon as she began, I noticed that many in

1. The veracity of this Kosinski anecdote has been the subject of much debate over the years. For specific information on the controversial nature of this and other Kosinski stories, see "Tate Did Expect Kosinski," *New York Times*, April 15, 1984, 35; James P. Sloan, *Jerzy Kosinski: A Biography* (New York: Penguin, 1997); "True Lies," *New York Times*, April 21, 1996, 16; "Lying: A Life Story," *Los Angeles Times*, May 12, 1996; "True Liar," *Chicago Tribune*, March 29, 1996.

the audience had a look of awe and discovery. At the reception after the performance, she stayed over so as to be able to converse with all who waited to meet her. In fact, she was the last one to leave. . . .

Before Queen Noor of Jordan presented her program "Women and Peace" at the Forum in 2005, I met by chance a young hotel official who happened to be a Jordanian. He was excited about Queen Noor's visit and had tickets to attend. I invited him to come to a post-performance private reception and introduced him to Queen Noor, who paid him particular attention. Later, he told me with some feeling, "I had to come to America to meet my queen." ("Poetic Moments")

There are many other memories, too, including Maureen Stapleton's decision to travel by train from New York to Pittsburgh and back because she wouldn't fly "even on Air Christ"; Lynn Emanuel's anecdote about a blonde "so blonde" that she inspired a poem; [and] Eva Marie Saint's reply when asked how she would prefer to die—"Quickly, but not today" ("Poetic Moments").

In a February 13, 2009, *Post-Gazette* interview, Edward Ochester, a poet, emeritus professor of English at the University of Pittsburgh, and editor of the Pitt Poetry Series at the time, said, "In starting the forum, [Sam Hazo] was the person who created the first element of the poetry renaissance in Pittsburgh... It's really remarkable, and he did it with an enormous amount of energy for raising money and getting things going... What Sam did certainly spread to inspire poetry readings at Pitt, Carnegie Mellon, Chatham. Pittsburgh is now a center of poetry in the United States. It's a sad loss" ("Poetry Forum Utters Its Final Verse").

Lynn Emanuel, director of the Pittsburgh Contemporary Writers Series and professor of English at the University of Pittsburgh, added, "The poetry forum is the father of all of us. Sam and the IPF were what started it all. I don't know how many reading series there are in the city now, but frankly without them, I doubt that very many of us would be doing what we are doing. Sam managed to maintain an extraordinary quality throughout the whole program. He really set the bench mark for the rest of us" ("Poetry Forum Utters Its Final Verse").

Although he recalls positive experiences with most of the forum's performers, Hazo assessed a handful of famous poets as complete fakes. Despite their reputations as excellent poets, Hazo wasn't fooled. "It took their appearance at the Poetry Forum to convince me that they weren't poets at all," Hazo maintains. "So many people wouldn't have noticed because they take other people's word for it that so-and-so is a poet. But you know when you've heard something that touches you. Everybody knows that. Anyway, a couple of them—including John Ashbery—weren't poets at all in my estimation. He had won all the awards—the National Book Award, etc. but I'm not impressed by his work."

Most of the poets and performers, however, were kind and genuinely talented professionals who graciously shared their gifts with the people of Pittsburgh. Reflecting on what he believed to be the forum's most valuable contributions over its forty-three-year history, Hazo says:

Well, I hope that it gave a platform for poetry—that it made poetry part of public discourse. So that when someone said they were going to a poetry reading, it didn't sound like they were going to someone's basement. [He laughs.] That's the first thing. Secondly, I think it exposed a lot of people to the art of listening. I had many high school students tell me that they learned how to listen at the Poetry Forum. Third, it made poets of note accessible to people who would otherwise never have seen them, never have talked to them, never have met them. And I think the last thing is it exposed people to how the American language sounds in the hands of people who take it very seriously.

Supporting Hazo's efforts for the forum's duration, of course, was Mary Anne—the one who encouraged him to pursue the idea in the first place. Mary Anne was (and remains) the absolute love of Sam's life, essential in every respect—as best friend, lover, parenting partner, travel companion, career advisor, and advocate.

MARY ANNE HAZO

In all matters, the two were one: "For those / who love, the sum of one / plus one is always one" ("Twenty and Not Counting"). Beyond her kindness, wisdom, and perceptivity, however, Mary Anne possessed an extraordinary quality that Hazo appreciated for its almost magical powers: her ability to recognize beauty and see the hand of God in all people and things. Hazo does not always share this gift, so he was gratified by Mary Anne's capacity to identify and reveal goodness and beauty—even when hidden. In the following excerpt from "Mary Anne's on Any Anniversary," he extols the effect she has on others: "Darling, no wonder / every child and flower opens up / to you. / You can't be unreceiving / or deceiving if you want to, / and you've yet to want to. / That's your mystery."

The image of flowers opening up to Mary Anne is more than a poetic device; it was a reality. A magnificent gardener, Mary Anne assembled and conducted a symphony for the eyes. Using a time-specific strategy, she planted various flowers in the front and back of their Upper St. Clair home so that each would bloom at a different time of the year. The result, of course, was a yard bursting with different colors and shapes in all seasons. "Her yard was all hers," Hazo explains. "And she didn't take flowers for granted. Even when a plant or flower looked dead and most people would have given up on it, she could bring it back to life. She tended them very carefully. One night she sat in that chair [pointing to a chair in their living room] with an orchid next to her. Completely happy just keeping company with the orchid." Through years of witnessing Mary Anne lovingly tend her garden, Hazo learned the names of the flowers and which ones would bathe their yard in brilliant color each season. With their yard as her canvas, proof of Mary Anne's artistry was always as close as the nearest window.

Hazo's love poems to Mary Anne often convey his belief in God's mysterious presence in their lives. Their union is sacramental, blessed, divine, and in the following poem, even sanctioned by the flowers.

The Vow We Breathe

It's not the years.
What
are they but a way (and not
the best) to count the past?
And what's the past but who
we've grown to be right now?
And how can that make life
more sacred or an inch
less dangerous?
Our rooms
gaze out on flowers that proclaim
like flags we're here to be
each other's counterpart, and that's
enough.
And yet to live
together but to die alone
seems so unjust of God
the merciful.
The mate who's left
goes on but partially, unable
or unwilling to disguise the naked
limp of being incomplete.
The Greeks were wrong.
Those
whom the gods would destroy
they make at first not mad,
but happy.
What else
is tragedy, is life?

                    If I
could make a toast, I'd say
each breath and not each year's
an anniversary.
                    Your rhododendrons
say that every time they bloom.
And so do all your hyacinths,
azaleas, tulips, dogwoods,
lilacs, and wisterias.
                    Because
of you I bless these blossoms
by their names.
                    I bless this true
and holy earth that undergirds
us while we live and hides
us when we die.
                    I bless
all love that baffles understanding,
human or divine.
                    What else
explains how every mate's
a lock one key alone
can open?
                    I'm yours.
                    You're mine.

In this prophetic poem, the poet envisions a future without his love by his side and momentarily questions God's justice and mercy. Working through his doubt, the poet comes to realize that the heartbreak of losing his mate will stem from the immeasurable joy he experienced with her by his side—the years of blissful union. Thus he ends "The Vow We Breathe" with an affirmation of his faith in God and a blessing on the flowers, the holy earth, and "all love that baffles understanding / human or divine."

Among the many gifts Sam and Mary Anne shared, one of the most satisfying was their ability to interpret their different temperaments as marital spices that added excitement and flavor to their relationship. Although they always agreed on "the basics," their approach to more trivial matters differed widely. In "The Thrower and the Keeper" (excerpted below), Hazo paints a picture of a couple that all readers can recognize, employing a lighthearted tone to demonstrate how opposites attract and complement each other:

From The Thrower and the Keeper

I claim the Iroquois were right—
    "Travel light, travel far."
                        You say
    the things we chuck today
    we just might need tomorrow.
So here we are—the chucker
    and the saver, now against
    mañana.
                On trips you pack
    for three eventualities—delay,
    disaster and demise.
                        I pack
    the clothes I plan to leave
    behind, the socks I'll never
    wear again, the books
    I bring to give away . . .
                    To be exact,
    you're two-thirds right.
                    When I
    need dimes for tolls or parking
    meters, presto! you produce
    them from the pocket of your coat.

If I need dollars, presto! out
   they pop like Kleenex from the selfsame
coat.
      And that trick works
with any coat.
         You keep
a history of birthdays, wedding
dates and anniversaries, and twice
that saved us from the worst
of all embarrassments.
           You store
for years the sales receipts
I'd throw away, and once
that spared us a calamity.
         I doubt
we'll change.
        What leaves me edgy
makes you more assured, so why
adjust?

And in the next poem, Hazo again highlights their counter-points:

From Mary Anne's on Any Anniversary

      I hate fast
and love slow while you're
the opposite.
        I'm Centigrade.
You're Fahrenheit.
          I throw away
You treasure.

> I hear the words
> and trace the silhouettes.
>   You learn
> the rhythm and enjoy the colors.

Despite these differences, though, the partnership worked because they stood united on the important matters: "I do my best to thank you / for your bravery of heart, your sense / of who'd be hurt by what / is said or left unsaid, your rage / when something totally unjust / is totally ignored" ("The Thrower and the Keeper"). And the poet cuts directly to the heart of the matter when he answers the question, "What bonds us then?" in "Mary Anne's on Any Anniversary": "A love of figure-skating, / manners, courage, and the poetry / of being kind? / Or just / that difference makes no / difference to the heart."

Hazo describes love as "the most powerful force in human existence." But genuine love cannot and does not exist without sacrifice and a willingness to change:

People who are willing to be changed by love literally create their lives all over again daily. Some people think they are capable of loving somebody without change, forever, and without sacrifice. They believe they don't have to work at it. That's a happy romantic thought, but it's not true. In order to demonstrate the love that you have for your family or your children or your mother, it's just not enough to say it. There must be some kind of action—and it has to be something that is done at some sacrifice to you. That's the proof of it. In the Christian religion the final proof of love is to lay down your life for your friend. At your most human moments, you realize that someone else's life means as much to you as your own—or in some cases, more than your own life means to you. If you have a feeling that your love is close to that, that's a pretty good proof you're a lover. (Hazo qtd. in Sokolowski, 245)

That is precisely the kind of love that Sam and Mary Anne shared—a powerful, transformative love that he appreciated as a daily miracle. Every moment spent with Mary Anne was a gift to Sam, and he immortalized those moments not only in poetry but also in his journal. He writes, "The final and only truth is that I love Mary Anne. If being only half-there when she's away is a proof of love, I love her. If not wanting to see her hurt in any way is a proof of love, I love her. If being certain of her being there when life becomes most difficult is a proof of love, I love her. If dreading that she might die before me is a proof of love, I love her. What more can I say?"

The fear that Mary Anne would die before him manifests itself with increasing regularity in Hazo's later, more mature poems. In "Definitely," excerpted below, the poet fears the loss of his loved one more than death itself.

From Definitely

Knowing my wife's
in pain, depressed, or wronged
lets nothing matter more
until she smiles.
Love makes
whatever's threatening or risky
unignorable because finality
is always possible.
That leaves me
thoughtfully mortal.
For those
who have such thoughts, the fear
of loss exceeds the fear
of death itself.

The poem "In Troth," Hazo believes, most closely captures the essence of their love after many years of marriage. Hazo says he did not intend to write a love poem; instead, he originally intended to write about the pledge that couples make to one another. But when he started writing about fidelity, it all came to him in vivid snapshots of his life with Mary Anne. Thus "In Troth" is a deeply personal love poem to his wife, his true love, the one to whom his allegiance is so complete that he could not imagine life without her.

In Troth

Forget the birthdays.

For me

you're younger than ever.

Nothing

is truer than that.

Tonight

I thought of life without you,
and I died—no one to kid
or kiss, no one to say
that blue is not my color,
no one to shuck mussels with
from the same bowl, no one
to live the patience that is love
in waiting.

You're always new

to know—a mate I'd choose
all over every day.

You make

our lives seem one long day
with no past tense.

I love you

for the times you've slowed me down
before I would have blundered.

I love you for the hundred ways
    you saw what I would
    never see until you'd seen it
    first.
           We're nip and tuck,
    saddle and boot, a pair
    of gloves, a study in rhyme
    from A to Z without a flub
    between.
           We're grateful so
    for one lone son whose music
    loops the globe, grandchildren
    three, and Dawn who keeps
    all five in love together
    and intact.
           If I could make
    Right now eternal as a song,
    I would.
           Impossible, of course.
But not the wanting to . . .
                  That's why
    I want impossibility to last,
    regardless.
           That's happiness.

The author begins this poem by envisioning an empty, lonely future without his beloved, where he has "no one to kid / or kiss, no one to say / that blue is not my color, / no one to shuck mussels with / from the same bowl." Finding this vision too painful to bear, however, the poet shifts to more joyful thoughts, offering a litany of reasons for loving her, a reminder of how well they work together, and a nod to their son, daughter-in-law, and grandchildren, for whom they are both so grateful.

But the poem ends with the reality of time's progress, the last few lines delivering a heart-wrenching message. Here the poet presents a hypothetical wish that their lives could stay exactly the way they are at that moment for *eternity*: "If I could make / Right now eternal as a song, / I would." Immediately, he acknowledges the futility of such a wish, but he refuses to let go of the desire for their lives to stay the way they are *at that moment* because, quite simply, "that's happiness." The anguish of the poem stems from the juxtaposition between the poet's knowledge that his desire is an impossibility and his refusal to abandon it.

Like "The Vow We Breathe" and "Definitely," "In Troth" turned out to be a crushingly prophetic poem. After a protracted and heartbreaking illness, Mary Anne died on Thursday, July 7, 2016. During her illness, Hazo devoted his full attention to caring for and being with her. Although he certainly didn't disappear from the literary scene for those eight years, he accepted far fewer speaking invitations, and he temporarily slowed the pace of publication. Despite a devastating diagnosis of dementia, Sam and Mary Anne both remained strong and hopeful—which Hazo attributes entirely to Mary Anne's fortitude: "Mary Anne had a built-in hope about life that made me stronger even when things seemed to be at their worst," Hazo says. "She never cried, she never griped, she never felt sorry for herself. She had more courage than I could imagine, and she never lost that courage. She was simply totally brave about everything."

Despite the incontrovertible truths—that Hazo made sure Mary Anne had the best doctors, that he stayed by her side, loved her, and took care of her every need for those eight years—Hazo believes now that he didn't do enough for Mary Anne during her illness. In a conversation eleven months after her death, Hazo said, "I want to tell you something, and I don't want to go on with this—but until I die, I will feel that I could have done more, much more. And done better. I wanted to do more, but I didn't know how." In retrospect, of course, Hazo realizes he was in denial about Mary Anne's disease. Until the end, he believed that, with the right care and motivation, Mary Anne would recover and be restored once again to her former vibrance and good health. Unconsciously and unintentionally, therefore, Hazo rejected both the claims of medical science that dementia has no cure and the conversations with the doctors and his son and daughter-in-law encouraging him to accept the inevitable.

His refusal to accept the painful truth, Hazo believes, caused him to make decisions that were detrimental to his beloved wife at the time. He says, for example, "If I had accepted it, perhaps I wouldn't have forced her to walk as much as I did, or maybe I would have been a little more patient. I was too much the marine—trying to tough it out." He did not acknowledge the need for safety rails on their bed until Mary Anne fell out of bed one night and could not get up. And he did not safety-proof their front door until Mary Anne wandered out of the house and down the street at dawn one morning while Hazo was still asleep. "That's what I mean," Hazo explains. "I could have been more alert to what could go wrong. [My son] Sam was much better at that. He knew medically that there were dangers, and I didn't accept them until I absolutely had to." Naturally, Hazo's state of denial was rooted in his deep love and commitment to Mary Anne, but that fact does not provide any solace now. Hazo continues:

Even if you try to understand and accept it, dementia is a terrible disease—very unpredictable on a daily basis. It wasn't something that happened overnight. Some days and entire weeks, Mary Anne felt great and seemed fine, and that gave me hope. One of the reasons I like to look at older photographs is that I want to see her when she was in her prime, not when she would forget things or have trouble walking, or not recognize me. Things like that.

When asked if that happened frequently, Hazo responded, "It happened enough to know that it happened. And it's hard to forget those things." Sitting on his couch surrounded by family pictures on every available surface, Hazo shakes his head as he looks at one of the pictures on the side table. In it, he is dancing cheek-to-cheek with Mary Anne, both beaming genuinely blissful smiles. "All I can say is that I was the luckiest man in the world. I have never met a better person in my life."

Mary Anne's funeral took place three days after her death, on what would have been her ninetieth birthday. In "One Another's Best," Hazo addresses his deceased love: "My only one, my dearest, / your requiem and birthday / happened together." But instead of falling into despair at the cruelty of the coincidence, Hazo instead poses a question filled with faith and hope for their eventual reunion: "Was this / your way or God's of promising / that right now and forever / would someday be the same / for us, regardless of the odds?"

Approximately one year after Mary Anne's death, Hazo honored her in an unpublished essay titled "For Mary Anne, But Moreso." Partially excerpted in the following paragraphs, the lines reveal a man who has experienced the despondency of grief at its deepest level and ultimately found comfort in his Christian faith. Christianity—in particular the very life and death of Jesus Christ—confirms for Hazo a continued union as well as hope for reunion with his beloved wife:

From "For Mary Anne, But Moreso"

Mary Anne [was] God's gift to me. We were one in all ways for the sixty-three years we were given to share. But her death was a separation only in a physical sense. I no longer had someone near me to care for or care. But I've learned that love buries death inasmuch as my longings and feelings for her have not diminished but intensified. Sometimes I am so overcome by my feelings that I have to stop whatever I am doing and compose myself.

I have long since accepted the fact that so many aspects of our lives are rooted in unity—the need for unity. People who suffer from neurotic or psychotic disorders experience a temporary or permanent breakdown of personality—a disunity in themselves. Through counseling and other aids, they are helped to re-discover their unified selves. I suspect that one reason we return for reunions of any kind (such as the reunion of my class at Notre Dame) is that we desire to reunite with a time in our lives when we began to turn into our true selves. We want more than to be reminded; we want to be reunited, to be made one with it again. We see examples of this in everything from literature to baseball. It took Odysseus twenty years to return from Troy to Ithaca, but the hunger to rejoin his wife and son never let him rest until he saw them again. It may seem a far leap from the Odyssey to baseball, but there is a connection. In baseball, the batter at home plate has no higher goal than to return to home plate—to go from home to home. He even runs counterclockwise around the bases as if to emphasize that time does not matter in baseball. Reaching home comes first.

I see in such goings and returnings the very essence of our sojourn on this earth. We have prefigurings of this in our return to old neighborhoods or houses where we once lived. It's the same impulse that draws us to old photographs of ourselves or friends or family members. We are reunited with our past that suddenly becomes present again. This is more than nostalgia. It is an inner drive to discover the unity within our changing lives.

Applying this impulse to marriage, I see a parallel. Marriage begins with a voluntary union of a husband and wife. This is followed by an intimate communion during their years together and, after one is taken, the hope in the survivor for an eventual reunion. The love that death cannot and does not kill strengthens this hope. It is even evident in the very life of Christ. In his becoming the Son of Man, He proceeded from union with God the Father to His incarnation (becoming flesh), then to three and a half decades of communion with His parents, friends and followers and finally to His eventual death by crucifixion and reunion with God the Father.

This is not an abstract theological principle to me. I've already stated that love buries death. This is affirmed by the demonstrable fact that death cannot kill the love that mates have for one another. On the contrary—and I speak personally here—that love is actually strengthened in the mate who survives. If these feelings are universally felt by the living for the beloved dead, it strikes me as contradictory and even perverse that a loving God would instill them in us only to have them proved illusory.

Speaking in human terms, I believe that a living person's devotion to one loved but taken would somehow help redeem that person's understandable grief at the loss. Believing in an eventual reunion would keep the survivor's life from degenerating into despair. The hope of reunion—and, yes, it is a hope—would motivate the survivor to live a life worthy of such a reunion and, if proved true in a life after death, make any sacrifice or act of forbearance more than worth the dedication and effort. It would be reassuring to know in advance that this reunion is based on knowledge, but it is not. It is singularly based on hope—the vital love-strengthened presence of hope. This is all we have in wishing for an eventual reunion.

Such a hope for reunion for mates is more profound than the wish to be reunited with family members no matter how strong those bonds may be. The love for our parents, grandparents, uncles, aunts, cousins, brothers or sisters is beautiful and singular in its own way, but these are loves that are traceable to chance. The love of spouses is based on choice and is ultimately more intense because it is voluntary. In this sense the love of my Aunt Katherine for my brother and myself was a love based on her choice to raise us. Even though we were related, her choice to raise us was not obligatory. It was derived from a vow that she voluntarily made to our mother. We became in a sense the children that she never had, and she became the mother we never had. This has always meant to me that the "greater love" that is praised in the New Testament is a love of choice. It is usually taken to mean that someone sacrifices his life for his friend, i.e. actually loses his life. But should it not also include dedicating one's life out of love for the good of others on a day-to-day basis?

In Mary Anne I found and saw what human beauty means. It was not only physical beauty although I can truthfully say I never saw a more beautiful woman. Moderately tall, she walked with an erectness that never seemed forced. Her ultimate beauty was in her face—her eyes especially, her smile, the way her jaw would flex determinedly when she made up her mind. Hers was a thoughtful beauty totally devoid of vanity. Each time I see her face in a photograph, I am suddenly with her again. But something is missing. Even though her presence is real to me then, I miss her physical presence. This is as inevitable as it is expectable. Despite my belief in the spirituality of love, I miss looking at her up-close, embracing her, holding her hand, kissing her or feeling my cheek next to hers. Hers is an absence for which there is no anodyne, no compensation, no end, no substitute. I loved, admired and revered her, and I do so still and always will. But this ironically confirms how important the physical presence of someone loved is. Octavio Paz was simply and profoundly true when he wrote that human love is Eucharistic. Lovers are truly one another's sustenance. What else could John Donne have meant but that when he wrote: "Love's mysteries in souls do grow, / But yet the body is his book."

One can never know in advance how one will react to the death of someone dear. Pre-thinking and anticipation are inevitable but futile. The sense of loss that death creates in turn creates a void that can be explained or defined in no other terms but the fact itself. In a poem I wrote years ago entitled "The Ballad of the Old Lovers" the following line appears: "In touch or apart is the same to the heart." If losing a mate is painful to the survivor, this only proves that the love was true. They stay in touch. If suffering is the price we pay for accepting this legacy, that is what life exacts. Gratitude and hope confront the pain, but they do not subdue or reduce it. Nothing really does. Nothing else can.

This essay poignantly articulates Hazo's profound grief at the loss of his beloved, but it also demonstrates an extraordinary capacity to intellectualize his feelings, ultimately formulating a cogent philosophical position regarding death. Absence, he argues, becomes activated as presence, and we must take comfort in that presence as we journey from physical union to spiritual reunion with our deceased loved ones. This evolution from physical union to absence, then presence, and ultimately reunion, Hazo asserts, was modeled for us two thousand years ago by Christ's death and resurrection.

Hazo explores the concept of "presence" in a poem titled "Alone with Presences," written during Mary Anne's illness.

Alone with Presences

Paying my tax bill can wait.
Some huckster hawking condos
  in Belize can leave a message.
King Death can keep his terrors
  to himself for once.
                              I live
    by preference in space where clocks
    have no hands, and time
    is what it is when there is
    nothing else to think about.
Infinity takes over long enough
    for me to reunite with those
    I loved the most.
                           It eases me
    to feel they're near, which proves
    those gone are never gone.
I play backgammon with my father
    in a dream and lose and lose.
I'm talking Plato with my brother
    in Annapolis.
                        It's then and now
    where FDR and JFK stay
    quotably alive while Marilyn
    Monroe survives and thrives
    in all her blonde availability.
Are these as everlasting
    as my aunt's devotion or my mother's
    smile when she sang or how
    my brother faced his last
    Epiphany without a whimper?
Who says that those who've gone
    are ever out of sight or mind?

> They're present but invisible.
>   They visit
>   when they choose.
>   They rule the world.

The final line of the poem serves as the title of Hazo's 2016 collection *They Rule the World*. Mature and reflective, these poems undeniably convey Hazo's preoccupation with the passage of time and our own mortality. In "Alone with Presences," Hazo contemplates the power and purpose of both conscious memory—which sustains us and helps us cope with the loss of our loved ones, and unconscious memory—the manifestation of memory in our dreams. It is, he claims, as close as he has ever come to writing a personal credo—an insistence that we are more the creatures of space rather than time. He explains:

> It has been said that memory is the cemetery of the mind, but sometimes it's a very living cemetery. And my point here relates to our Christian experience of the Eucharist, too. The Eucharist is our way of embracing Christ while we're living. We understand it as a living presence, and it sustains us, but it also parallels our human experience of remembering those who are dear to us. We do it involuntarily, but it's unforgettable. Presence is eternal and always, and the poem is finally an affirmation of the existence of matters spiritual that are capable of influencing us for the better.

Although "To Mary Anne, But Moreso" and "Alone with Presences" eloquently outline Hazo's spiritual philosophies regarding immortal presence, the poems that he wrote after Mary Anne's death deliver the most powerful emotional impact. Not surprisingly, the postmortem love poems express many of the same themes that Hazo conveys in the essay above, that is, absence and presence, feelings of loneliness and despair, and the role of Christian faith in our grieving and healing process. Unlike the more steady and cerebral essay, however, the brutal honesty and raw human emotion of the poems lacerate—often thrusting the reader into a stunned silence. In the poems, we see a man bereaved of his raison d'être and struggling to find meaning or even "one ounce of dignity" in the life he has now been sentenced to endure without his beloved.

In "God's Gift to Me," a poem that Hazo wrote just three months after Mary Anne's death, he addresses his deceased wife in the present tense as if writing her a love letter or engaging her in a personal conversation. We learn immediately, however, that the passing of time since her death has brought him no reconciliation and no relief.

God's Gift to Me

My dearest Mary Anne,
    I'm no more reconciled
    than I was three months ago.
You're everywhere I look—
    from raincoats hangered
    in a closet to framed photographs
    to car keys for a car
    you never drove.
                I sleep
    and wake now on your side
    of the bed . . .
                To say that other
    men have lost their wives
    is no relief.
                Devastation
    stays particular and merciless
    if shared or not.
                Longevity
    offers nothing but more
    of the same or worse . . .

                                    I miss
         your face, your voice, your calm
         defiance in your final months,
         your last six words that will be
         mine alone forever.
                                 Darling,
         you were my life as surely
         as you are my life today
         and will be always.
                                We're close
         as ever now but differently.
         "Why do we have to die?"
         you asked.
                          I had no answer.
         My answer now is rage
         and tears that sentence death
         to death each day I wake
         without but always with you.

Here the poet rejects the idea that "time heals." It has been
three months since his beloved wife's death, and the ubiquitous
reminders of her throughout their home provide no succor. He
also rejects the platitude that misery loves company ("other men
have lost their wives"), stating that "Devastation / stays particular and merciless / if shared or not." He confesses that he longs for
her *physical presence*, laying bare his need to see, hear, and touch
her: "I miss your face, your voice, your calm / defiance in your final
months, / your last six words that will be / mine alone forever."
    The final thirteen lines of the poem reveal the poet's intense
internal struggle to become reconciled with her death. On the
one hand, he feels overwhelmed by emotions of despair and anger; on the other hand, he acknowledges that he and Mary Anne
are still together and always will be, just in a different way. The

fervency of the conflict between competing forces is brilliantly conveyed by its positioning on the page—first, a concession that she is with him eternally: "Darling, / you were my life as surely /as you are my life today / and will be always. / We're close /as ever now but differently." The poet is mercilessly jolted out of this seemingly comforting acceptance, however, by a memory of his beloved's agonizing deathbed question: "Why do we have to die?" His inability to answer her question brings back his anger and despair: "My answer now is rage / and tears." The ultimate poetic skill comes into full force in the final stanza that begins with the poet's rage and tears but then shifts clearly yet seamlessly three times, expertly articulating the poet's internal struggle: "My answer now is rage / and tears that sentence death / to death each day I wake / without but always with you."

As it turns out, his rage and tears ultimately give dignity to his grief by sentencing "death to death each day"; that is, his love conquers death. But the tension in the final line reveals his ongoing difficulty as he attempts to move toward an acceptance that her spiritual presence has replaced her physical presence: "each day I wake / without but always with you." He initially rejects spiritual presence as a sufficient substitute for the physical reality of his beautiful wife—although he wakes up each day *without* her, he uses the final four words of the poem to accede: "but always with you."

Hazo wrote the following poem several months after "God's Gift to Me":

One Night at a Time

You kept the outcome at a distance
    with your smile, but the end
    was scripted in advance.
                        Each time
    our eyes locked, the tears
    came.

I had to turn away.
You held my hand—the left.
Each night in what passes
   now for sleep, I wake
   to learn how absence crucifies.
Nothing compares with it.
What can I do to give
   this grief an ounce of dignity?
Only the ache of not having
   you beside me brings you
   back and keeps you close.

The poem begins with the speaker, still grieving deeply, haunted by the vivid memory of his courageous beloved in the late stages of illness. Although he initially seems inconsolable: "Each night in what passes / now for sleep, I wake / to learn how absence crucifies," the poet soon reveals that his anguish *is* the path to redemption and healing: "Only the ache of not having / you beside me brings you / back and keeps you close." Here the grieving widower is made to feel whole again only by the excruciating pain caused by his deceased wife's absence. In "God's Gift to Me," absence transcends the physical world, becoming spiritual presence that the poem's speaker acknowledges but cannot bear to accept completely. "One Night at a Time," however, illustrates the poet's spiritual acceptance, as the pain caused by his beloved's absence actually redeems and saves him.

The motif of "absence as presence" appears in several other poems and essays that Hazo wrote after Mary Anne's death. In the essay included earlier in this chapter, Hazo writes: "But her death was a separation only in a physical sense. I no longer had someone near me to care for or care. But I've learned that love buries death inasmuch as my longings and feelings for her have not diminished but intensified." And toward the end of the essay, he says, "If losing a mate is painful to the survivor, this only proves that the love was true. They stay in touch. If suffering is the price we pay for accepting this legacy, that is what life exacts." In the poem "Stages," the poet assures his beloved: "Because you're with me always, / I'm never alone," and in "Nightly," he affirms his "trust in love ongoing / from time present into presence. / I'm grateful for seven hundred / and fifty-three months I shared / with Mary Anne and share still, / share now."

Perhaps the next poem, written more than a year after Mary Anne's death, however, most clearly demonstrates the poet's ultimate acceptance:

> *From* One More Year, One Year Less
>
> Without you I am sentenced
> to myself.
>   The house we chose
> together has a past that's always
> present: Waterford glasses
> you treasured, sunflowers
> you brought from Cannes and vased,
> the sculpture Starchev gave you
> after you praised it.
>   They help me
> feel you're near.

Unlike the raincoats, framed photographs, and car keys that only caused him pain in the beginning ("God's Gift to Me"), the household items that remind the poet of his beloved now help him to feel that she's near. In the next stanza of "One More Year, One Year Less," the poet lovingly remembers his wife's genuine smile:

> In photographs
> you smile as my bride, my wife,
> and later as a mother hugging
> three grandchildren on our sixtieth.
> Never forced or false, your smile
> was everywhere and always
> *you.*
> Each day for more
> than sixty years that smile
> saved me.
> And saves me still.

As evidenced by this and all of the poems written after Mary Anne's death, Hazo endured a tortuous period of grief and anguish. But through the pain—the ache of her absence—he ultimately found a path to acceptance and hope. James Matthew Wilson, poet and editor of Hazo's collection *When Not Yet Is Now*, says:

[Hazo's] chief abiding theme—a reconception of time, the past, as contained within the space of the present—has reached new depths because of its elegiac reflections on loss ... His poems of elegy for his wife and reflections on his own mortality are themes for which a poet who has always been concerned about the nature of time can be expected to have a certain authority in undertaking. He has that authority." (interview, January 18, 2019)

Perhaps more than anything else, Hazo's Christian faith helped him to move through the grieving process—which he asserts will be ongoing for him—and come to a full acceptance of Mary Anne's death. His faith, in fact, provided exactly what Hazo needed: hope for an eventual reunion with the love of his life. The excerpt from the next poem, which Hazo wrote prior to Mary Anne's death and included in her requiem mass program, clearly illustrates this belief:

From The Renegade

> After thirty-three
> years of breath and three days
> of death, the Messiah rose
> to resume living with those
> He loved.
>
> Compared with that,
> who needs theology or ritual
> for reassurance?
>
> What's truer for God
> or each of us than unions
> resurrected as reunions?
>
> What else
> is faith but trusting that loves
> once known will be known forever?

We see the same argument in "For Mary Anne, But Moreso":

It is even evident in the very life of Christ. In his becoming the Son of Man, He proceeded from union with God the Father to His incarnation (becoming flesh), then to three and a half decades of communion with His parents, friends and followers and finally to His eventual death by crucifixion and reunion with God the Father.... This is not an abstract theological principle to me.... Speaking in human terms, I believe that a living person's devotion to one loved but taken would somehow help redeem that person's understandable grief at the loss. Believing in an eventual reunion would keep the survivor's life from degenerating into despair.

If not comfort, exactly, Hazo certainly found in Christianity a way to go on living without Mary Anne—not despairing and not merely existing—but living a life worthy of an eventual reunion with her.

In the years since Mary Anne's death, in fact, Hazo has absolutely lived a life that would make Mary Anne proud. At the time of this writing, he has published seven new books: *Outspokenly Yours* (2017, prose); *The Pittsburgh That Stays within You* (2017, memoir, updated); *The World within the Word: Maritain and the Poet* (2018, prose); *When Not Yet Is Now* (2019, poetry); *The Power of Less: Essays on Poetry and Public Speech* (2019, expanded edition); *If Nobody Calls, I'm Not Home: The Open Letters of Bim Nakely* (2019, fiction); and *The Next Time We Saw Paris* (2020, poetry). He has also published multiple poems and essays in journals and newspapers, and remained busy with poetry readings.

One additional poem deserves mention here—a poem celebrating the most cherished qualities of married love. Titled "Conjugals," this recent poem signifies Hazo's ability to universalize the deepest feelings he shared with Mary Anne for all married couples, which clearly indicates continued healing of his broken heart.

Conjugals

Each one is the other's only
    other, and so they mate
      without impatience or pretension.
Kisses are their secret language.
Their differences dismiss what
    difference means whenever
    they embrace.
            They have the gift
    of making imperfections perfect,
    and thoughts of death ignorable.
Parted by necessity or fate,
    they'd feel like amputees.
The fear of that returns them
    to themselves.

> Nothing
> must come between them.
> And nothing can or will
> undo their perfect fit.
> Together they complete each other
> solely for the need of it.

Hazo does not ever foresee a public recitation of the poems he wrote for Mary Anne. "Frankly, I don't know what would happen to me if I started saying them," Hazo says. "I wrote them specifically for her, and I can't tell you why, but I feel that it would cheapen them if I said them in public."

In 2018—at the age of eighty-nine—Hazo accepted an invitation to serve as the inaugural poet-in-residence at La Roche University. Reconnecting with his classroom roots in this position, he taught several poetry courses and gave guest lectures in various classes throughout the college. Of the La Roche experience, Hazo says, "I enjoyed every aspect of the residency. It was both refreshing and rewarding to be back in the classroom. There's not a substitute for backing-and-forthing with students." As a fitting conclusion to the esteemed poet's residency, La Roche faculty organized an appreciation event called "Sam Hazo—A Circle of Friends," which consisted of a poetry recital by Hazo followed by a book signing and farewell reception. Students, faculty, staff, and community members packed the Kearns Spirituality Center for the event, and Hazo received a rousing, standing ovation at the end of his reading. Although he enjoyed every aspect of the residency, Hazo admits that "Having the chance to crown it off with the poetry recital at the end was the whipped cream on the sundae."

In 2019, Hazo received yet another high distinction when he was nominated for the position of US poet laureate. Written and submitted by Washington, DC, attorney Mark Paoletta and me, the nomination also received endorsement letters from several acclaimed poets and authors, including Mike Aquilina, Dana Gioia, Jo McDougall, James Matthew Wilson, and Ryan Wilson. Although Joy Harjo was ultimately appointed to the position, the solid support Hazo received from his contemporaries must surely have made the decision a difficult one.

When asked which professional endeavors he presently finds most satisfying—writing, reading, teaching—Hazo explains that they are all rewarding in different ways: "Dialogue with students is finally what education is. Working out a poem is always dramatic and always a mystery, i.e., where it came from, what the right word is, when to stop. You work really at the behest of the poem." In other words, he enjoys it all and shows no signs of slowing down in the foreseeable future.

And while Hazo was working diligently on all of these ventures, he was simultaneously dedicating countless hours to this literary biography—generously sharing stories, memories, philosophies, and ideas over a period of three years and granting access to personal journals, files, photographs, and poetry forum archives, all of which deeply enhanced this author's understanding of his life and work.

SIX

Silence Spoken Here

The name of the game was destruction
in the time of the tumult of nations.
We knew we were once better people
in the time of the tumult of nations.

"In the Time of the Tumult of Nations"

I f we grant that the subjects of interest to a poet will be much
broader than the limited range of topics we are likely to en-
tertain in our own lives, it can be said that the poet's canvas is as wide-ranging as the human condition. All issues, ideas,
or institutions that affect, enhance, degrade, or compromise humanity are concerns that are ripe for a talented poet to reveal and
clarify in verse for us. Unlike the previous chapters, which have
sought to highlight significant people, moments, and events in
Hazo's life, this chapter reveals some of the recurrent attitudes,
philosophies, and themes in his work. His pen vividly depicts the
subjects he deeply cares about. In the process, he leaves us with
profound, sometimes humorous, and always truthful insights
that can offer us hope for humankind.

War

Hazo's disdain for "presidentially chosen" wars—their destructive impact on individuals, nations, and institutions—is evident in his poetry and prose alike. In a compelling essay titled "O Say Can't You See," Hazo considers what our country has become over the course of the past fifty years, outlining some key "regressions" that have contributed to our present state of affairs. Hailing back to the 1980s and the economic policies of the Reagan administration, he reminds the reader that the population of middle-class citizens experienced a steep decline during that decade while the rates of those living in poverty rose dramatically. Consequently, young men who were unemployed and couldn't find work joined the military "with its promise of the G.I. Bill and sizable bonuses for extension. This in turn enriched the pool of servicemen to be committed to another presidentially chosen war" (*Outspokenly Yours*, 169). A military composed solely of willing volunteers, Hazo explains, "assures compliance without dissent." Unfortunately, this phenomenon of a shrinking middle class continues today. Add to this the present reality of skyrocketing higher education tuition, and we see that "only the wealthy or those resigned to a lifetime of debt can cope with collegiate costs" (170). According to Hazo, the result is scores of young people who continue to choose military service as their first step on the path toward a college education—which ultimately ensures a military brimming with men and women who stand ready to support the next presidentially chosen war. This, Hazo argues, makes endless war not only a possibility but a grim reality.

In an essay titled "The War Within," Hazo elaborates on the appalling monetary, human, and societal costs of these wars:

Since the end of World War II, every administration has in varying ways been involved in war. The only one that was presented to Congress for its approval and support was the Persian Gulf War. George H. W.

Bush asked for and received Congressional approval (albeit by only a few votes) to turn back the Iraqis from their attack on Kuwait. All other wars, i.e. Korea, Lebanon (twice) Grenada, Vietnam, Afghanistan and Iraq, were "declared" unilaterally by the President. The cost in dollars was in the trillions and counting. The cost in the lives of American men and women in the military is approximately 85,000. As for wounded Americans, the number in Vietnam alone is 8 times the 58,000 killed. Veteran suicides average 22 per day. The total of Koreans, Vietnamese, Afghans, and Iraqis killed is astronomical. In Vietnam alone the deaths of North Vietnamese exceed 2,000,000 while South Vietnamese losses range around 1,000,000, including those who were left to the tender mercies of the Vietcong after we left. In Iraq, more than 500,000 civilians have been killed, and that's a conservative figure....

The historian William L. Cohn has written: "Endless war is the destruction of civil society." All we have to do is look at what's become of American society since 2003 to see how true this is. As a people, we have become more militaristic, more and more concerned with security, more intolerant of dissent, more top-heavy with wealth controlled by the oligarchic few and more inured to death by violence than we have ever been. We average 80 homicides per day compared to 13 this year in Japan (where owning a gun or a sword is illegal), and annual murder rates are proportionately lower in other countries as well: Norway (29), Greece (93), England (549), Spain (363) and Switzerland (57). Comparatively speaking, these annual totals seem paltry when placed against our total of homicides in 2017, which was over 28,000.

Hazo calls upon historians and scholars—namely, David Wood (*What Have We Done: The Moral Injury of Our Longest Wars*), Michael Chabon and Ayelet Waldman (*Kingdom of Olives and Ash*), Robert Reich (*The Common Good*), and Tony Judt (*Ill Fares the Land*)—to support his claim that a state of endless war causes society to decay both morally and spiritually. "As a people and as a government," Hazo says, "we are now less altruistic, more self-concerned, more acquisitive and less generous" than we were in the past.

Hazo's poetry articulates his revulsion just as powerfully as his prose. "Soldiers Despite Ourselves" captures the essence of his contempt for all wars and ends abruptly—on a note of uncharacteristic hopelessness:

Soldiers Despite Ourselves

Downstairs a trumpeter is playing
    Gershwin badly but somehow
    truer that way.
                The squat
chimney of my pipe keeps offering
    smoke signals to the moon.
The sea-waves glitter like a zillion
    nickels . . .
            Two wars ago
    the battle of the Riviera happened
    here.
         Two wars ago
    the author of *The Little Prince*
    flew southward from this coast
    and crashed at sea without a trace.
That's how I tell the time
    these days—by wars, the madness
    of wars.
        I think of Mussolini,
    who believed each generation
    needed war to purify its blood.
He leaned on history to show
    that life's unlivable except
    through death.
          I palm the ashes
    from my pipe.

                              To hell
            with Mussolini.
                              I'll take
            bad Gershwin to a bullet
            any time.
                              To hell with history.
            The moon's manna on the sea
                outshines the glory that was Greece.
            To hell with those who say
                the earth's a battleground we're doomed
                to govern with a gun.
                                        Because
                of them we have to fight to live.
            But win or lose, they've won
                since fighting proves they're right.
            Why ask if they outnumber us
                or not?
                              It just takes one.

Hazo says the idea he talks about in that poem really bothers him because it's so true. "You can believe in nonviolence," he explains, "but it will have no effect whatsoever. As long as one person disagrees with you, you'll have to surrender completely or fight like hell." When we discussed this poem, Hazo had recently read a book contending that Adolph Hitler was the most significant man of the twentieth century in terms of world change. "As much as I did not want to accept that, I had a hard time disagreeing with the author," Hazo says. "And what bothers me the most is that since WW II, the U.S. has become a militaristic country. The Pentagon has the largest public relations budget of any government or fiscal institution in the world."

The following two poems offer scathing indictments of the American war machine through agonizing personal portraits of two veterans—the first, a former marine who must now adapt to life with only one leg, and the second, a former army sniper who suffers with severe and untreated posttraumatic stress disorder. Hazo wrote these poems as ballads because he enjoys the rhythm and appreciates the honesty of the ballad format. "The high point of Elizabethan and English poetry started off with the balladeers," Hazo explains. "There's a very interesting connection between a story and a verse, a tale and a song. Originally, of course, the ballads were sung." The juxtaposition of content and form in these ballads contributes to the powerful emotional response they elicit, as the rhyming verse contrasts starkly with the devastating story told in each ballad.

Ballad of the One-Legged Marine

For Ray Fagan

My left leg was gone with the boot still on—
the boot that I laced in the morning.
I felt like a boy who had stepped on a toy
and made it explode without warning.

They choppered me back to a medical shack
with no one but corpsmen to heed me.
I stared at the sky and prayed I would die,
and cursed when the nurse came to feed me.

I knew that I must, so I tried to adjust
while orderlies struggled to teach me
the will of the crutch and the skill of the cane
and assured me their methods would reach me.

The President came with his generals tame
and explained why he never relieved us.
But the red, white and blue of my lone, right shoe
told the world how he lied and deceived us.

They buried my shin and my bones and my skin
an ocean away from this writing.
But pain finds a way on each given day
to take me straight back to the fighting

when I served with the Corps in a slaughterhouse war
where we tallied our killings like cattle
as if these explain why the armies of Cain
behave as they do in a battle . . .

Whatever's a bore, you can learn to ignore,
but a leg's not a limb you like leaving.
So you deal with regret and attempt to forget
what always is there for the grieving.

If you look for a clue while I stand in a queue,
you can't tell what's real from prosthetic.
I walk with a dip that begins at my hip,
but I keep it discreet and aesthetic.

If you're ordered on line and step on a mine,
you learn what it means to be only
a name on a chart with a hook in your heart
and a life that turns suddenly lonely.

Lose arms, and you're left incomplete and bereft.
Lose legs, and you're fit for a litter.
Lose one at the knee, and you're just like me
with night after night to be bitter.

As the dedication indicates, this poem was written in honor of
Ray Fagan, a fellow Notre Dame alumnus and officer in the Marine Corps when Hazo was an enlisted man. Like many of Hazo's
fellow marines, Fagan was deployed to Korea, but after only one
week, he stepped on a mine and lost his leg. Back home in the
United States, he fell in love with the nurse who cared for him in

the hospital. They married and had seven children. Although Hazo met Fagan before his deployment and heard about his military-career-ending injury, they did not maintain contact after the war. Strangely enough, however, a young woman approached Hazo after he recited this poem at a University of Pittsburgh reading one evening. The woman told Hazo her name was Cheryl Fagan and that she believed the poem was about her father. After a brief conversation, it became clear that the Ray Fagan of the poem was indeed Cheryl's father. She confessed experiencing a strong emotional reaction upon hearing the poem because—although she and her siblings obviously knew about their father's prosthetic leg—he always refused to talk about it. Their mother told them how the accident occurred, but Ray "just never mentioned it." Hazo's poetic envisioning of what Ray must have endured: the physical and psychological pain as well as the feelings of betrayal, loneliness and bitterness, significantly impacted his daughter.

The next poem addresses an equally pernicious type of battle injury: posttraumatic stress disorder.

Ballad of a Sniper

This is the way that it happened.
This is the way it was done.
The boy was the son of a hunter,
and his father gave him a gun.

Each day until he was twenty
he slowly perfected his aim.
It was something he did as a hobby,
and his targets were never the same.

War came, and he went to the army.
They noticed how well he could shoot.
They trained him to fly with commandos
and jump with a parachute.

His job was to pick off the leaders
of enemy troops by surprise.
He tracked them like prey in his gunsight,
and the crosshairs were surer than eyes.

By the time he became a civilian
he thought he'd forget what he learned.
He tried to adjust to his family,
but he left and never returned.

He went from one job to another
but never could settle on one.
He felt that the world was against him,
and all he could trust was his gun.

He locked himself high in a tower
and targeted people below.
They told him to throw down his weapon.
His answer in bullets was no.

Debating his ultimate choices
of yielding his rifle or not,
he peered down the muzzle and kissed it,
then reached for the trigger and shot.

    This poem was partially inspired by a horrific mass shooting at the University of Texas at Austin on August 1, 1966. After stabbing his wife and his mother to death, former marine Charles Whitman armed himself with rifles and other weapons and began shooting people at random from the observation deck of the main building's tower on campus. He killed sixteen people and injured thirty-one others in 90 minutes before he was shot and killed by police. Although an autopsy revealed that a brain tumor was the likely culprit for the violent fantasies and impulses he had been experiencing—and for which he had sought professional counseling before the shooting—Hazo uses the incident as a departure point to explore the effects of untreated posttraumatic stress disorder.

Societal Ills

Although war figures prominently in Hazo's work, it is far from the only societal ill he addresses. In the next two poems, "Overtime" and "In the Time of the Tumult of Nations," the poet argues that all is not well with the world today as we feed on a steady diet of violence, inept leaders, fear, insecurity, lost appreciation for genuine art, and watered-down intelligence. The result: a general, sickening sense of malaise, moral decline, and societal decay.

Overtime

It's much too late to think
    of options or alternatives.
Our Pharaoh-in-Chief is waiting
    like a spoiled prince for loyalists
    to kiss his ring.
                    Meanwhile
the little we have saved is taxed
for war.
            No one admits
we've made a hoax of peace
by living behind closed doors
and stashing dollars for the worst.
We're drunk with ultra-security,
    ultra-speed, ultra-vitamins,
    ultra-power.
                We converse
through machines.

                          We think
        in slogans.
                  We worship glitz
        and notoriety.
                        We choose novels
        for "easy reading."
                          As for poetry?
        It's all reduced to wordplay
        and sociology.
                        Meanwhile
        the televised and tattooed world
        slides by disguised as normal.
        We sit and watch.
                          Even
        when seated, we keep a pistol
        holstered at the hip and ready.

Hazo masterfully employs concepts of the past and present tense in the next poem, initially leading the reader to believe that he is reflecting on a time in our nation's distant past. Explaining his handling of past events in his poetry, Hazo says, "The past can't be ignored because it happened. So, when you write about past things, you have to be merciless on yourself. You can't doctor up the events to make yourself look good or make the situation different than what it was." In this poem, however, Hazo's employment of the past tense does little to stanch the forceful bleed into the present as the reader confronts a stark reality.

In the Time of the Tumult of Nations

We thought that the worst was behind us
    in the time of the tumult of nations.
We planned and we saved for the future
    in the time of the tumult of nations.

The crowds in the streets were uneasy
    in the time of the tumult of nations.
We murdered our annual victims
    in the time of the tumult of nations.
We were fined if we smoked in the cities
    in the time of the tumult of nations.
We gave and deducted our givings
    in the time of the tumult of nations.
We kept the bad news from the children
    in the time of the tumult of nations.
We wakened from nightmares with headaches
    in the time of the tumult of nations.
We voted for men we distrusted
    in the time, in the time, in the time,
    in the time of the tumult of nations.

In the time of the tumult of nations
    the ones who were wrong were the loudest.
In the time of the tumult of nations
    the poets were thought to be crazy.
In the time of the tumult of nations
    the President answered no questions.
In the time of the tumult of nations
    protesters were treated like traitors.
In the time of the tumult of nations
    the airports were guarded by soldiers.
In the time of the tumult of nations
    young women kept mace in their purses.
In the time of the tumult of nations
    the rich were exempt in their mansions.
In the time of the tumult of nations
    we waited for trouble to happen.
In the time of the tumult of nations
    we lived for the weekends like children.

Like children we clung to our playthings
　　in the time of the tumult of nations.
We huddled in burglar-proof houses
　　in the time of the tumult of nations.
We said that the poor had it coming
　　in the time of the tumult of nations.
We readied our handguns for trouble
　　in the time of the tumult of nations.
We tuned in to war every evening
　　in the time of the tumult of nations.
We watched as the bombs burned the cities
　　in the time of the tumult of nations.
The name of the game was destruction
　　in the time of the tumult of nations.
We knew we were once better people
　　in the time of the tumult of nations.
We pretend we are still the same people
　　in the time, in the time, in the time,
　　in the time of the tumult of nations.

Although the first few lines of the poem seem to refer to some distant past, it quickly becomes clear that the time of the tumult of nations is indeed our present reality. According to Hazo, "We have become people now who are overtaken by events: events of war, mass murder, terrorism. The journalists all rush to cover these events and interview everyone, but of course nobody has a clue why these events occurred." The poem, Hazo says, is a reaction to America as it *should* be. He reflects on the first years of the twenty-first century:

The first decade of this century was for me one of the lowest points of my life as an American. Our government's reaction to the horrific slaughter on 9/11 was to opt for further slaughter via lies, presidentially-chosen wars, propaganda, and so on. Prophecy has been correctly defined as seeing not the future but the present. If I had to choose any poem of my own that I would consider prophetic in this sense, it would be the litany of this poem. This is the only poem I have ever written that came to me in this way—a series of accusations with every accusation followed by a thematic line that is repeated like a drumbeat. The rhythm of accusation after accusation linked by these identical drumbeats creates almost a sense of outrage when the poem is read or heard.

As a side note in our conversation, Hazo mentioned that audience members applaud every time he recites this poem. "They never applaud anything else during the reading because, well, you don't applaud during poetry readings. But when I finish this, they applaud. I think they all feel a little this way."

Time and Happenstance

Concepts of "time"—how we understand it, why we feel so compelled by it, what we learn from its passing, and many related ideas—figure prominently in Hazo's poetry. As one of his primary poetic themes, "time" makes its way into so many of Hazo's poems that he dedicated his 2014 collection of poems (*And the Time Is*) to it. Although each of the following four poems ponders separate notions regarding time, the deeply *spiritual* nature of time exists at the heart of each. The title poem to the collection follows:

And the Time Is

We have come to the point of decision,
    and the hands of the clock say—be careful.
We've learned from the past that our choices
    are one or the other or neither,
    and the hands of the clock say—be careful.

We have readied ourselves for the challenge
   by weighing the odds and the chances
   of what will result from our choices,
   and the hands of the clock say—be hopeful.

We're not what we were when we started,
   and the hands of the clock say—it's over.
Our yesterdays lengthen like shadows
   that fade when we no longer cast them,
   and the hands of the clock say—it's over.
Despite what it brings to surprise us,
   we treasure each day in its passing
   though we know that we pass as it passes,
   and the hands of the clock say—discover.

We sit on the porch every evening,
   and the hands of the clock say—be watchful.
We study the leaves in their turning
   from green to vermillion to purple,
   and the hands of the clock say—be watchful.
While we stare at the sky in its vastness
   and name every star in the distance,
   we dwindle to scale in the balance,
   and the hands of the clock say—be grateful.

The dead come to life in our dreaming,
   and the hands of the clock say—remember.
The words of a prophet keep haunting
   the ones who ignored him when living,
   and the hands of the clock say—remember.
The world that we think is around us
   is neither before nor behind us
   but always within us, within us
   and the hands of the clock say—forever.

This poem captures the essence of Hazo's philosophy of life in just four stanzas. The first stanza deals with life as a series of decisions. We create a life for ourselves and hope that we make the right choices. He says:

The second stanza reminds us that life passes, and we can't live on memories alone. When people get to the point where they're convinced that everything is over, something in us says, "Look around. Discover. See things differently," and we do. Then we encounter the question of both memory ("The dead come to life in our dreaming") and the need to decide where our life is at that moment. We realize ultimately that the real world exists "neither before nor behind us / but always within us." And that's the world that lasts forever—the world that exists within our hearts. It's spiritual.

Inspired when the line "and the hands of the clock say—" came to him, Hazo started to contemplate the clock as a kind of "death count." Always marching forward, we often become preoccupied with time: What can we accomplish in various blocks of time? How can we strategize for optimal efficiency? How should we assess portions of our lives that have passed? But clock time, Hazo insists, is artificial time: "We only *really* live when we live in space, not time. Real time is when we are growing or learning or experiencing something that contributes to our human development. Pregnancy is real time. Traveling is real time. There's a deeply spiritual difference between living in time and living in space."

Hazo admits that of all his poems, "this one gives me the greatest satisfaction. It somehow covers the human lifespan, embracing choice and memory, attention and forgetfulness, now and forever." He adds that this poem completely possessed him while he was writing it, presumably because it conveys his personal philosophy of life. Although it's not the poem that took the most time to compose or offered the greatest technical challenges, it held his attention—to the exclusion of all other writerly concerns—until it was finished.

The title poem of Hazo's 1996 collection *The Holy Surprise of Right Now* explores our tendency to live for the future instead of savoring, as the poet suggests, the feast that is *today*. Americans, Hazo argues, tend to prioritize the future as the only important aspect of time—"But I don't believe in the future," Hazo insists. "I think the future holds every bad or good thing that can still happen to you, but that never preoccupies me."

The Holy Surprise of Right Now

If you can see your path laid out ahead of you step
by step, then you know it's not your path.
—Joseph Campbell

Inside Brooks Brothers' windows
    it's July.
               Sport shirts on sleek
    dummies speak in turquoise,
    polo, Bermuda and golf.
Outside, it's very much the first
    of March.
           The sport shirts say
    today's tomorrow and the present
    tense be damned.
              They tell me
    to forget that here's the only place
    we have.
            They claim what matters
    most is never now but next.
I've heard this argument before.
It leaves me sentenced to the future,
    and that's much worse than being
    sentenced to the past.
              The past
    at least was real just once . . .

                                                            What's
          called religion offers me the same.
     Life's never what we have
          but what's to come.
                                        But where
          did Christ give heaven its address
          except within each one of us?
     So, anyone who claims it's not
          within but still ahead is contradicting
               God.
                         But why go on?
     I'm sick of learning to anticipate.
     I never want to live a second
          or a season or a heaven in advance
          of when I am and where.
     I need the salt and pepper
          of uncertainty to know I'm still
          alive.
                         It makes me hunger
          for the feast I call today.
     It lets desire keep what
          satisfaction ends.
                              Lovers
          remember that the way that smoke
          remembers fire.
                              Between anticipation
          and the aggravation of suspense, I choose
          suspense.
                    I choose desire.

Religious allusions pervade the lines of this poem—starting
with a consecration of the present in the poem's title. Clearly,
the poet is urging us to understand and appreciate our present
reality as a gift from God: "But where / did Christ give heaven its

address / except within each one of us? / So, anyone who claims it's not / within but still ahead is contradicting / God." Although the overarching message of this poem differs significantly from the life philosophy espoused in "And the Time Is," the spiritual dimension they share confirms the poet's belief that each moment of each day is divine.

"A Time of No Shadows" contemplates the interconnectedness of time, space, and immortality, suggesting that our translation from the physical "here" to the spiritual "hereafter" could be as simple and instantaneous as a drive across the state border:

A Time of No Shadows

Immortality?
                    Too general a concept.
Some say it's never-ending time,
        which means it's long on myth
        but short on meaning.
                            Some say
        it's never to be known until
        it's ours.
                    Some say, some say . . .
I stand with those who think
        it could be quick as any instant
        going on and on and on
        within itself like poetry or music
        or a kiss.
                    That comes as close
        as anything to God's *"I am
who am."*
                    No past.
                            No memory.
No future but the time at hand
        that's passing even as it's born . . .

Once I was driving due southeast
through Pennsylvania.
                                    Highways
were broad and dangerous and everyone's.
As I ran out of Pennsylvania,
farm by farm, I noticed
border signs that welcomed me
to Maryland where Rand McNally
said that Maryland began.
I knew the earth was still
the earth in Maryland or Pennsylvania.
I knew I stayed the same,
border or no border . . .
                                    From here
into hereafter could be just
like that—our selfsame selves
translated instantly from state
to state to God alone
knows what . . .
                    That's immortality.

Here time collapses, "going on and on and on / within itself like poetry or music / or a kiss," and the immediacy of the transition to immortality "comes as close / as anything to God's 'I am / who am.' / No past. / No memory. / No future but the time at hand / that's passing even as it's born." A deeply spiritual contemplation of the afterlife, this poem was inspired in part by the line "I myself am Heaven and Hell" in the "Rubáiyát of Omar Khayyám." Hazo does not believe that heaven and hell exist as places; instead, they are conditions that we can experience even before we die: "If you suffer from something you've done, if you have regret or guilt, that's hell. After all, your conscience is supposed to be the voice of God within you. But if you get an intimation of happiness that just takes over, that's heavenly." Connecting ideas of hope, eternity, and the power of love, Hazo expounds upon his philosophy in his essay "When Clocks Have No Hands," originally published in the Spring 2019 issue of *Pittsburgh Quarterly*:

The ultimate virtue of hope is what ought to motivate us to live charitably together until that time when life for each of us is not taken away but, in the coda of many religions and biographies, changed. Those who have lived a loving life hope to discover that death is trumped by love because love does not die when the person dies. Instead love intensifies. For me this has always been the existential guarantee of most religions, namely, that the gift of faith in a life hopefully lived and motivated by love (or kindness to) others is a preview of immortality. To be reunited in eternal love is the fulfillment of that hope.

Time adopts a slightly different purpose in the following poem, as it unites with notions of body, sense, and death in a poignant demonstration of interrelatedness that we often fail to recognize.

Who Promised You Tomorrow?

It's time you paganized yourself
    and left all sublimations
    to the dry of soul.
                It's time
    you learned that ears can taste,
    and eyes remember, and the tongue
    and nostrils see like fingertips
    in any dark.
           Think back
    or look around, and all you know
    is what your body taught you:
    lake smoke in the Adirondacks,
    the razor's flame across
    your lathered cheek, language
    that changed to silence or to tears

when there was nothing more
to say . . .
                    Right here in Cannes
on the Fourth of July, you watch
a cornucopia a-swelter in the sun.
A Saudi wife, enrobed
    and cowled like a nun, passes
    a Cannaise in her isosceles
    and thong.
                    They stand there
    like opposed philosophies of women,
    history, desire, God,
    and everything you think about
    too much . . .
                    The stationed candles
    on the altar of Notre Dame
    de Bon Voyage diminish
    like your future.
                    Anchored
    in the bay, the S. S. *Ticonderoga*
    claims the future's now.
Housing a zillion dollars'
    worth of hardware in her hull,
    she's programmed for the war
    that no one wants.
                    She bristles
    like a ploughshare honed into a sword—
    the ultra-weapon from the ultra-tool.
Basking in the hull of your skin
    that shields the software of yourself
    against the worst, you contemplate
    the carefully united states
    you call your body.

                                        Concealed
    or bared, it houses who you are,
    and who you are is why you live,
    and why you live is worth
    the life it takes to wonder how.
Your body's not concerned.
                                    It answers
    what it needs with breath, sleep,
    love, sweat, roses,
    children, and a minimum of thought.
It says all wars are waged
    by puritans, and that the war
    nobody wants is history's excuse
    for every war that ever happened . . .
The gray *Ticonderoga* fires
    a salute of twenty guns
    plus one for independence
    and the men who died to earn it.
Each shot reminds you of the killed
    Americans still left in France.
Before they left their bodies,
    did they think of war or what
    their bodies loved and missed
    the most: a swim at noon,
    the night they kissed a woman
    on her mouth, the times they waited
    for the wind to rise like music,
    or the simple freedom of a walk,
    a waltz, a trip?
                        Under
    the sun of Cannes, you hum
    your mind to sleep.

                                        You tell
        yourself that time is one
        day long or one long day
        with pauses for the moon and stars,
        and that tomorrow's sun is yesterday's
        today.
                        Your body answers
        that it knows, it's known
        for years, it's always known.

   "Well . . . who promised you tomorrow?" Hazo asks. "What human being can say with conviction that he'll be here in five minutes from now?" In this poem, Hazo adopts Miguel de Unamuno's
perspective on life: that we can only appreciate life if we develop
a tragic sense about it, because the worst can happen to any of us
at any time, regardless of our disposition. We adhere to certain
values that we deem important, but we do so in a world that is
governed by chance. Hazo asserts, "The good do die young, not
because they're good but because they contracted pneumonia,
because they drowned, or because they stepped in front of a car"
(qtd. in Sokolowski, 253).

Chance

In his personal journal, Hazo explains the significance of chance
in his own life:

Most if not all of the important things that have happened to me in my
life have been a matter of luck, i.e., receiving the scholarship to Notre
Dame, becoming a Marine Corps officer after I'd enlisted as just an ordinary "grunt" (I had no way of knowing that the Corps would open up
an officer's program for enlisted men who were college graduates.)—my
meeting Mary Anne—our having a son after ten years of marriage and
all kinds of doctoring (to this day, nobody can explain how Mary Anne's
pregnancy occurred just once when she was almost 40 and how there

wasn't the faintest whiff of a pregnancy before or after that)—the creation of the International Poetry Forum, and so on. All of these crucial and defining moments in my life were quite outside of my control. They happened to me, and their happening created my life. This leaves me thinking that chance has as much to do with our lives as choice, and perhaps that is how it should be.

"By Chance" demonstrates how events that "happen without acclaim / or notice" often develop epochal status in our lives:

By Chance

It seems too minor to mention—
　　　the day a Frenchman found
　　　my car-keys in Provence and refused
　　　a tip.
　　　　　　"Pour la France," he said
　　　and smiled . . .
　　　　　　　　Or how my son
　　　at seven braved the bees
　　　to bring me Windex to defend
　　　myself against them.
　　　　　　　　　　My thanks?
"Get back inside right now . . ."
Or Monk who saved his nephew's
　　　life by giving him his kidney.
"I just need one," he said . . .
Or how Mary's adopted
　　　daughter from St. Petersburg
　　　played college soccer in Pittsburgh
　　　and kept no memory of Russia . . .
Or when that total and forever
　　　nameless stranger saved
　　　a six-year-old named me
　　　from drowning in the Adirondacks . . .

What happens without acclaim
or notice shows me how
a ship that's spotted by a man
marooned alone for years
can almost civilize the sea.

Inequities and Societal Pressures

Society's propensity to neglect admirable people and deeds finds its way into several of Hazo's poems. In "No Is the Father of Yes," he admits that "The causes / I believe in rarely win. / The men and women I admire / most are quietly ignored." When he wrote the poem, one of the examples Hazo was thinking about was Abraham Lincoln's stepmother, Sarah Bush Lincoln.

Three years subsequent to her first husband's death, Sarah married Thomas Lincoln, who was widowed with two children, Sarah and Abraham. She moved to Lincoln's Indiana farm with her three children, and they successfully blended their families. Sarah Bush Lincoln taught Abe how to read and write, and she gave him *Aesop's Fables*, Bunyan's *Pilgrim's Progress*, and the King James Version of the Bible. "Think about it for a minute," Hazo says. "Without her, he could never have been a lawyer; he could never have been president. And if he hadn't been president, we wouldn't be the country we are. All because of this woman who only received about one page of commentary in his biography and whom most people don't know anything about."

Hazo also believes the gender divide can be blamed for the lack of approbation many women receive. "When women help someone they care about, they don't want it known," Hazo posits. "Men want an airport named after them. They want their name on a stamp. They want a statue. I mean, just look at all these statues of men. Women don't care about all of that. As long as the person they love benefits from it, that's the reward."

"No Is the Father of Yes" also reveals the poet's annoyance with society's constant endeavors to influence our behaviors:

From No Is the Father of Yes

I'm tired of living for tomorrow's
　　headlines, tired of explanations,
　　tired of letters that begin "Dear
　　patriot . . ." or else "You may
　　already be the winner of . . ."
I'm near the point where nothing's
　　worth the time.

This frustration hails back to "The Holy Surprise of Right Now": "They claim what matters / most is never now but next. / I've heard this argument before. / It leaves me sentenced to the future, / and that's much worse than being / sentenced to the past. / The past / at least was real just once."

Clearly, after experiencing a lifetime of societal pressures, Hazo has had enough. In "What Ever Happened to Defiance?" he proposes a delightfully devious solution:

What Ever Happened to Defiance?

People you will never want to know
　　are telling you to vote, enlist,
　　invest, travel to Acapulco,
　　buy now and pay later, smoke,
　　stop smoking, curb your dog,
　　remember the whale and praise
　　the Lord.
　　　　　　　Like windshield wipers
　　they repeat themselves.
　　　　　　　　　　　　Because
　　they tell but never ask, you learn
　　　　to live around them just to live.

You understand why Paul Gaugin
   preferred Tahiti to the bourgeoisie
   of France.
                 But then Tahiti's
   not the answer anymore,
   and frankly never was.
                        This leaves
   you weighing Schulberg's waterfront
   philosophy: "You do it to him
   before he does it to you."
Reactionary, you admit, but nature's
   way, the way of this world
   where he who wins is always
   he who loses least and last . . .
But if you're bored of triumph
   through attrition, imitate you may
   the strategy of Puck.
                          Listen
   carefully to all solicitations, smile
   and respond in classical Greek.
It's devious, but then it gives
   you time to smell the always
   breathing flowers.
                       Or to watch
   dissolve into the mystery of coffee
   the faceless dice of sugar
   cubes.
            Or say just how
   remarkable it is that every
   evening somewhere in this world
   a play of Shakespeare's being staged
   with nothing to be won but excellence.

So long as we live and breathe in modern society, we will be subjected to other people's ideas regarding what we need. So Hazo believes we could all have some fun if we adopted a Puck-like response to marketing solicitations. "If someone calls you on the phone or knocks on your door and you speak in classical Greek to him, he's not going to stay long."

In addition to marketers constantly trying to sell us what we didn't know we needed, we are burdened by even more insidious pressures: to be wealthy, beautiful, popular, and successful; to be the winner "who loses least and last" and climbs the corporate ladder to the top. In "Ballad of the Jolly Broker," Hazo denounces the false glamour and allure of money:

Ballad of the Jolly Broker

Nothing was surer amid all the furor
than watching a stock that I picked on a hunch
make rich men of paupers, and paupers of fools,
and all in the pinch that it took to eat lunch.

My betting and cheering took real engineering.
I guessed and I gauged and I bet and I prayed
from the dawn of the bull to the dusk of the bear
where fortunes were waiting and fortunes were made.

The world of percents is a world that resents
whenever its buyouts are less than a steal.
Its language is numbers, and numbers are lethal,
and all that makes sense is the luck of the deal.

You have to like poker to be a good broker.
You have to take chances and hope for the best.
Buy cheap and sell dear is the law of the market,
and woe unto those who forget or protest.

Like any good broker I loved to play poker,
but poker's a gamble where all that you've got
is the lure of the cards and the stack of the chips
and the dice of the draw and the pay of the pot ...

I took all my winnings that some called my sinnings,
and lived like a king where the snow never fell.
I drank all my juices and swallowed my pills,
and bet on the races, and down came hell ...

It cost me my wife in the prime of my life.
It made me content with much less than the best.
I worked for the day when I never would work,
and the money was sure, and the honey was rest.

If you'd rather be healthy than feeble and wealthy ...
If you'd rather be happy than wed to a bed,
then think of a man with a millionaire's tan
who died half a lifetime before he was dead.

"You can quote that to your educators," Hazo says after reciting the poem. The blind pursuit of wealth without regard to one's
physical or mental health ranks high on Hazo's list of societal ills.
And it's exacerbated by institutions of higher learning that teach
young people the wrong priorities. In Hazo's estimation, students
are taught that the whole purpose of work is to create wealth so
they no longer have to work. "But that's a rotten ideology," he
says. "If you're doing what you love—which is what your education *should* prepare you for—you don't want it to end. What's
the use of amassing a fortune? What are you going to do with a
hundred and sixty-five million dollars a year?"

To Hazo, the soul-crushing race for riches damages us on both
the individual and societal level. But the quest for wealth is far
from the only threat to our souls. Hypocrisy and false religiosity
also rank high on the list of dangers, as "National Prayer Breakfast" suggests:

National Prayer Breakfast

Conventioneers from thirty-seven
   countries throng the banquet
   hall to hear the message.
A clergyman tells God to bless
   the fruit and rolls.
                 The President
   speaks up for Reagan, Martin
   Luther King, and having faith
   in faith.
           Love is the common
   theme, most of it touching,
   all of it frank, unburdening
   and lengthy.
               If faith is saying so,
   then this is faith.
                The problem is
   that I must be the problem.
I've always thought that faith
   declaimed too publicly destroys
   the mystery.
            Years back,
   when Brother Antoninus yelled
   at listeners to hear the voice
   of Jesus in them, Maura whispered,
   "The Jesus in me doesn't talk
   that way."
            Later, when I saw
   a placard bannering, "Honk,
   if you love Jesus," I thought
   of Maura's words and passed
   in silence ...

Jesus in fact
spoke Aramaic in Jerusalem,
foretold uninterrupted life
and sealed it with a resurrection.
If He asked me to honk
in praise of that, I'd honk
all day.
But rising from the dead
for me seems honk enough
since no one's done it since,
and no one did it earlier or ever.
Others might disagree, and that's
their right.
But there's an inner
voice I hear that's one
on one and never out of date.
It's strongest when it's most subdued.
I'll take my Jesus straight.

Hazo enjoys telling the story behind this poem. While Hazo
was in Washington, DC, on International Poetry Forum business
in 2003, his friend—a DC resident—asked if he wanted to meet
for breakfast. Hazo agreed, thinking it would be just the two of
them. His friend gave him the address, and Hazo found himself
at the National Prayer Breakfast with five thousand other people. "I can't stand political sanctity and political hypocrisy," Hazo
says with disgust. "George Bush was there, Condoleezza Rice was
there, Rick Santorum was there—everyone smiling and saying
'God Bless You.' You could cut it with a knife." Hazo explains why
he would not have attended the National Prayer Breakfast if he
had known what he was agreeing to:

To my knowledge, all of the founding fathers were Christian except Jefferson—he was an Agnostic. But the first thing they insisted on was a separation of church and state because they saw what the integration of institutions had done to Europe. So, they intentionally did not specify a state religion. Now, the fact of the matter is that you have a system of laws in this country—originating out of Natural Law, among other things—that are rooted in the Judeo-Christian religion, without using that word. To that extent, I'm persuaded that that's probably the only option because murder is murder, rape is rape, lying is lying, deceit is deceit, theft is theft, etcetera. Those who insist on putting Jesus Christ into government are doing exactly what the founding fathers said would be disastrous.

Although faith was certainly being "declaimed too publicly" for Hazo's personal tastes at the National Prayer Breakfast that morning, he had the pleasure of being seated with two of the event's scheduled performers. The first was country music star Randy Travis, who was met with great enthusiasm from the throng of five thousand. The highlight for Hazo, however, was a comedian named Jeff Allen who was so funny that he "made the whole trip worthwhile." On stage following Travis, the comedian opened with a great question: "How am I going to follow a guy who has twelve platinum records? I have one record with thirty-two copies sold to my family." That was the start of an act that "just broke me up," Hazo says with a laugh. "He was great."

Hazo recounts one bit from the act that he says he'll never forget. The comedian said he lives by a simple philosophy: Happy wife, happy life. He had been married for sixteen years and was very happy. One day, however, he came home after a bad day and was thoroughly disgusted. So he took off his shoes and socks and threw them on the floor. He took off his shirt and threw it on the floor. Took off his pants and threw them on the floor. Took off his underwear and threw them on the floor. He just tossed everything all over the bedroom floor on his way to the shower.

When he came out of the shower, his wife was standing there. He thought she would have told him to pick everything up, but she didn't. Instead, she looked directly at him and simply inquired, "Are these yours?" "If they're not mine, I have some questions of my own to ask," he retorted. So, despite Hazo's distaste for the otherwise sanctimonious climate in the room, the morning was rescued by some good jokes.

Silence

It seems somehow appropriate to end this chapter with silence—a concept that has captivated Hazo since his early days as a writer. In a poem titled "My Kings," first collected in his 1972 volume *Thank a Bored Angel*, silence speaks between the words: "Pauses between words / say all I want to say. / So, silence by silence / I give myself away." In his 1988 collection *Silence Spoken Here*, silence is much more than the absence of words or a moment of solitude. Instead, silence is what the words of a poem should evoke—"what their sound and heft and feel make palpable." After you hear a beautiful piece of music, see a play, or read a poem, sometimes you just want to sit quietly for a couple of minutes, Hazo suggests. You don't want to launch into conversation right away; you simply want to enjoy the silence the experience has created.

On the back cover of *Silence Spoken Here*, Hazo elucidates his theory on the relationship between poetry and silence:

If architecture exists to create space, poetry exists to create silence. Not mere quietude. Not solitude. Rather it is a silence within and by the experience of the poem itself. It inevitably exceeds the poem since, though the poem can create it, it cannot contain it. Within this silence the imagination and the feelings are renewed, and because of that renewal they live momentarily with a will and momentum of their own. In such a silence we are returned to ourselves, and we discover in ourselves the self that is common to us all. This silence is in essence our indispensable oxygen—the oxygen of our souls. If we try to communicate its presence to others, we do it best by not speaking at all, by letting the eyes convey it in that international language that is understood by all without translation.... Poetry then, being that ultimate conversational speech in which our love and suffering and hope find their voice, has no other purpose than to create those moments when silence can have its say.

Readers should be "plunged into silence" after they read certain poems, Hazo says, because "the ultimate poetry, if you are the perfect poet, is silence."

Hazo first started thinking about the creation of silence through art while he was reading *Hamlet* as a young man. With his very last breath, Hamlet says, "Oh, I die, Horatio... The rest is silence" (V.ii.336). Here, Hazo says, Hamlet's existence in that moment surpasses words; language cannot possibly express his thoughts or feelings, and that is precisely what moves the reader. He explains:

You live for a moment in that silence created by those words about silence. And in some cases the best lines ... are the ones that you hear between the actual printed lines. It's what's evoked by the space between words or the pause between sentences. The time a breath takes says more than what is said sometimes. So that's the kind of silence I'm talking about. It's a silence that is first of all created by experiencing a poem, and it's also the silence that we all live in when we're thinking about something that has overtaken us and subsumes us in itself." (qtd. in Sokolowski, 256–57)

Breath, pause, space, and silence converge in poetry to communicate what Hazo calls "visions of the inscrutable." As the universal language, silence is both spoken in Hazo's poetry and evoked by its message, as we experience in "Silence Spoken Here":

Silence Spoken Here

What absence only can create
    needs absence to create it.
Split by deaths or distances,
    we all survive like exiles
    from the time at hand, living
    where love leads us for love's
    reasons.
                We tell ourselves
    that life, if anywhere, is there.
Why isn't it?
              What keeps us
    hostages to elsewhere?
                    The dead
    possess us when they choose.
The far stay nearer than we know
    they are.
              We taste the way
    they talk, remember everything
    they've yet to tell us, dream
    them home and young again
    from countries they will never leave.
With friends it's worse and better.
Together, we regret the times
    we were apart.
              Apart, we're
    more together than we are
    together.
             We say that losing
    those we love to living
    is the price of loving.

> We say
> such honest lies because
> we must—because we have
> no choices.
>   Face to face
> we say them, but our eyes
> have different voices.

Beautifully expressing Hazo's philosophy of poetic silence, this poem presents a situation "that goes beyond words," according to the poet. "It presents a situation where no words exist to say what must be said. The implication of the very title is that silence is itself a language with a vocabulary that is not heard as much as it is sensed or felt. It is something akin to the silence that still exists after the poem is over. The poetry is in the silence."

To Hazo, love itself is a complete mystery—an enigma that resists definition and rational explanation and can only be understood through its "quiet proofs."

The Quiet Proofs of Love

When your son has grown up,
treat him like your brother.
—Arab Proverb

Don't wait for definitions.
                    I've had
my fill of aftertalk
and overtalk, of meanings that don't
mean, of words not true
enough to be invisible, of all
those Januaries of the mind when
everything that happens happens
from the eyebrows up.

If truth
is in the taste and not
the telling, give me whatever
is and cannot be again—
like sherbet on the tongue, like love . . .
Paris defined is Paris
lost, but Paris loved
is always Orly in the rain,
broiled pork and chestnuts
near the Rue de Seine,
the motorcade that sped de Gaulle
himself through Montparnasse.
Viva
the fool who said, "Show me
a man who thinks, I'll show
you a man who frowns."
Which
reminds me of Andrew, learning
to count by two's and asking,
"Where is the end of counting?"
Let's settle for the salt and pepper
of the facts.
Oranges don't parse,
And no philosopher can translate
shoulders in defeat or how
it feels when luck's slim arrow
stops at you or why lovemaking's
not itself until it's made.
Let's breathe like fishermen who sit
alone together on a dock
and let the wind do all
the talking.

            That way we'll see
      that who we are is what
      we'll be hereafter.
                  We'll learn
      the bravery of trees that cannot
      know "the dice of God
      are always loaded."
                  We'll think
      of life as one long kiss
      since talk and kisses never mix.
   We'll watch the architecture
      of the clouds create themselves
      like flames and disappear like laughter.

The final poem in this chapter, which Hazo wrote in the 1980s, contemplates the fundamental power of silence as the sacred mystery at the heart of love and religious faith:

The Courage Not to Talk

   Students may thank you for a word
      they say you said at the right
      moment.
               Nod and pretend
      you remember.
                  Nothing is lost
      by failing to be totally exact . . .
   A kiss from your son may stop
      you in mid-thought to prove
      that life is love or it's a waste.
   Be grateful.
                  Not everyone arrives
      at such assurances . . .

                                    Victims
        in Palestine may suffer on
        for being who they are.
                                    Recall
        the last beatitude whose prophecy
        is justice.
                        Something will change,
        and if you're not alive
        to see it, what's the loss?
Since gratitude and love and pain
        are languages you learn to speak
        by keeping still, keep still.
Silence has a million dialects,
        and every dialect's a mystery,
        and every mystery's a reason
        to be glad you're listening.
                                    Practice
        for mystery each night before
        you sleep.
                        Think past your eyelids,
        past the ceiling, past the roof
        and clouds and into spaces
        so immense that no geometry
        but God's can measure them.
Or else imagine you're about
        to die.
                        The words you want
        to say are hiding on the other
        side of death.
                            They tell you
        they're too sacred to be heard.
They say the only word
        you need to speak is breath.

SEVEN

Making It Look Easy

Like something born in hiding,
a poem lets itself be found
the more you fret and work
to free it of its flaws.

"A Poem's Only Deadline Is Perfection"

At the conclusion of an author's presentation, someone in the audience is sure to ask, "What inspired you to write this?" In reply, the author recounts a life-changing experience, a tragic event, or a person the author knew well—something or someone who inspired the poem or story. It may be true that such motivations exist for poets and storytellers. According to Hazo, however, genuine inspiration is altogether different from motivation. He explains that inspiration occurs when subjects "startle us into the present and keep us there as long as we are in their grip." The final chapter of this book is an intimate exploration of Hazo's view of the writing process as an interrelationship between poet and poem, an examination of his poetic technique, and ultimately an appreciation of Hazo's unique ability to be himself—boldly speaking his truth across more than sixty years as a poet.

Poetic Knowledge

Having published his first four volumes of poetry between 1958 and 1965, Sam Hazo was poised at the beginning of what would become a long and illustrious writing career when the journal *Humanitas* published his essay "The Poet and Society: Freedom to Create" in 1966. Although he was still a relative novice to the poetic community at that time, Hazo's prolific outpouring of publications in those first years quickly earned him a position as a respected voice in literary arts—and not just as a poet. By the time the aforementioned essay appeared, Hazo had already published several essays that explored connections between poetry, criticism, philosophy, and spirituality. His interest in these relationships began during his undergraduate study at Notre Dame and gained force during graduate school—ultimately culminating in his 1957 dissertation, "The World within the Word: Maritain and the Poet." In it, Hazo analyzed French philosopher Jacques Maritain's concepts of Art, Beauty, Poetic Knowledge, and Creative Intuition through the lens of aesthetic ideologies advanced by the great Romantic poets Samuel Taylor Coleridge and John Keats, and Victorian poet Gerard Manley Hopkins. Dedicating so much early study to the philosophy of art, Hazo began to develop his own deeply philosophical perspectives on poetry and the role of the poet in our world. His insightful 1966 essay "The Poet and Society: Freedom to Create" represented the foundation for what would remain Hazo's poetic philosophy for the next half century. In it, Hazo contemplated the societal responsibilities that inherently accompany poetic knowledge:

What is the real nature of poetic knowledge? How do poets know? According to most poets who have written on the subject, we can conclude that poets know without being fully able to account for this knowledge, except by testifying to it in their poems. They find it difficult to explain how they came to "know" a particular experience except to say that they received an insight, an illumination, an inspiration. The French Philosopher Jacques Maritain has constructed a complete aesthetic which attempts to give a rationale for this poetic experience. He has invented and defined terms like "knowledge through connaturality" and "creative intuition," but throughout his writings he does not deny the mystery inherent in the way poets know. They simply *know*, and although they know that they know, they cannot adequately account for it or prove it. From Plato's "divine madness" theory to recent essays by Allen Tate, Mark Van Doren and Robert Frost, the same insistence appears. The poet's knowledge is truly knowledge though beyond proof and often beyond accountability....

Since man is a creature who reaches his perfection through knowing the truth, and since the revelation of poetic knowledge is the poet's way of achieving this perfection, the experience of poetry is capable of perfecting men in the knowledge of truth. As long as men seek to know themselves and the world in which they live and move and have their being, poets will have something important to say to them. Poets will be there to remind them that knowing themselves is more than knowing their names, their weight and height and even their preferences. And ultimately, poets will be there to prove that most men don't know what they know until they try to say it or until they share it in a revelation of someone else who has said it as they might have wanted to say it....

This is the cornerstone of the poet's role in society. He is a man prompted to speak the truth in the way that he alone can and with the pleasure and power of which poetry is uniquely capable. But to be able to reveal this vision, the poet must be a free man—free in expressing what he truly knows, free in the exercise of his art, free in being faithful to his own vision. Only in the spirit of such freedom will the poet have anything valuable and permanent to say to men. "The freedom of the artist is like the freedom of the citizen," wrote Mark Van Doren in *The Happy Critic*, "he too must be left free to say in public what he thinks is true; suppress this right, and society suffers; suppress it long enough, and civilization dies." The relationship of the poet and society from the earliest documentations until the present moment may simply be the evolution of the implications of this single statement. (270–71)

Fifty-three years and numerous philosophical essays later, Hazo's fundamental views on poetic knowledge and the role of the poet remain consistent. He says:

I continue to believe that a poet is impelled to write because of inspiration—an insight or an impulse of feeling that will not rest until it finds its outing (for writers, that is) in words. The very act of writing is for the one inspired to find the words. In this sense writing is both a cooperative and a creative act. Jacques Maritain attributes the transformation of poetic knowledge into poetry through the power of creative intuition. Regardless of the terminology, the process is the same. In the broader sense as well as the spiritual one, the cooperative and creative act of writing parallels the creative act of God. Evolving a poetic inspiration into words that have been prompted by inspiration does resemble making something out of nothing. But it more resembles making something out of something else—a poem, that is, from words and images. What results does, of course, reveal the outlook or values or spirit of the author. But describing or defining that is for the reader or critic to determine, not the author.

As Hazo explains in the introduction to *The Power of Less: Essays on Poetry and Public Speech* (2019), an authentic poet is merely an apparatus through which the poems work their own particular magic:

The true poet, as Plato and Keats believed, is the instrument by and through which a poem is realized in a moment of insight or transport. In this sense, true poems are momentary epiphanies and they are invariably as brief as they are unforgettable. They startle us into the present and keep us there as long as we are in their grip. Like kisses or tears they have no past (or future) tense. Like telegrams they eschew the superfluous and value the vital—only the vital. They emphasize the power of less. This is not simply a matter of minimum word count. There are complete poems, to be sure, that are only one line long. There are others of many lines, but the lines spring from a single nucleus and have an equally singular focus throughout. The focus is what is important.

In this regard poetry stands opposed to those social forces that equate significance with "more-ness" or with what is bigger and better. It may seem like a contradiction to state that poetry is proof that, in artistic terms, less is more, but it is true. In their very succinctness poem after poem demonstrates this—no passenger words, no padding, no irrelevancies....

Ezra Pound once wrote that a poet was someone who, believing in silence, could not at times keep himself from speaking. If this is true, then poetry is akin to utterance. And utterance is more primordial than speech because it is nine-tenths involuntary—a gasp, a scream, an outburst like the "small white cries of love" that can no longer be contained. And often the briefer the utterance, the more powerful it is. A basic principle of physics applies here; that is, the more you reduce the volume, the more you increase the pressure. (x–xi)

For Hazo, inspiration for a poem springs from a variety of sources: "Sometimes it can be just two words that rub themselves together by accident," he says. Other times, it may be a vivid memory, a conspicuous irony, or simply a mood that he can't shake until he has explored its origin and given it poetic voice. Regardless of the origin, inspiration is essential to poetry.

Unlike many poets who have the discipline to write every day for a predetermined number of hours, Hazo must feel compelled by the poem. The process, for him, is entirely involuntary:

I've never been of the persuasion that poetry is something you do because you choose to do it ... A poem, if it's going to be any kind of poem at all, has to come and use you—hit you on the head. It also involves a certain reciprocity on your part. You may be wrestling with a particular ongoing subject that presents a dilemma to you, or creates a mood for you, and suddenly a poem comes to you that subsumes that, and then you're writing something on which, for the moment, the focus of your life depends, and it occupies all your attention for the duration of its inspiration and your refinement of it. I could quote Frost to you: "A momentary stay against confusion." That's what poetry is; it's a time when suddenly things come into focus, and you work under the imperative of some impulse, something you did not will into being, that came to you, and you must work it out in words that are just now coming to you, that are making you put everything that you have at that moment right on the line. (qtd. In Sokolowski, 259)

Hazo beautifully articulates this very phenomenon in the following 2019 poem:

To Happen

Arriving unforeseen and unexpectedly
as love, it never takes no
for an answer.
None who live
by rules or laws or clocks
can know how poems-in-waiting
happen.
Poets themselves
cannot explain it.
Inspired,
they feel obsessed and chosen.
They stay intact but incomplete
while trying to say as perfectly
as possible what must be said.
Afterward they realize
they had no option but compliance.
Even as they wrote, they wondered
how they'd written what they'd written
or if the words wrote them.

For Hazo, one benefit of longevity as a poet has been learning that when a poem does not come freely—when he has to will it into existence—it's probably not going to be very good. "You look at the poem, usually afterwards, and it just doesn't hold up. The only thing that held up was your interest in it and your tinkering with it, and your revising and correcting it. The *essence* of the poetry was not there right from the beginning. It's good to be able to recognize that kind of flaw more readily now." Although Hazo published a few of the forced poems when he was much younger and "too lenient on my own work," he would never do so now. Only the poems that continue to live for him maintain his interest. And the same is true for his poetry readings: "Unless a poem is still alive for me, I won't include it in a poetry reading. If it doesn't wear well with me, I just leave it go the way you leave go of old shoes."

This refusal to "force" a poem into existence could have become a stumbling block when Hazo was named Pennsylvania's first (and thus far only) poet laureate by Governor Robert Casey in 1993—a post he held for ten years. State poets, after all, are called upon to write and recite poems for special events and occasions. But Hazo understood that the position might require "poetry-on-demand," so he accepted the honor with the stipulation that he would not be paid. Naturally, if the post were absent financial incentive, Hazo knew he could decline special requests at his discretion: "I never wanted to have to write a poem for an occasion. Listen to the poets who speak at presidential inaugurations. The poems are often *terrible*. Elizabeth Alexander was asked by Obama to write a poem for his inauguration—and she wrote a very academic, awful poem. Poets are never at their best when their poems are forced."

In "Miracles Leave Doubts," Hazo explains the unforced poetry process through themes of Christian faith and conjugal love, as the personified poem demands to be written:

Miracles Leave Doubts

Prose I can will myself
    to write.
           It's always possible.

Poetry alone decides
　　when poems can be written.
The poems come all at once
　　or in stages.
　　　　　　　Jealous as love,
　　they leave no room for distraction.
A forced poem mimics
　　a forced marriage.
　　　　　　　Failure
　　is only a matter of time.
Even with geniuses, errors
　　are likely.
　　　　　　At fourteen years
　　could Romeo and Juliet
　　have known as deep a love
　　as Shakespeare said they knew?
Ignoring Emerson, were Whitman's
　　litanies of Americana nothing
　　but inventories?
　　　　　　　Who can explain
　　how Richard Wilbur wrote
　　better than the Elizabethans
　　five centuries later?
　　　　　　　And what
　　of Housman who felt past forty
　　what men of twenty feel?
Somehow the poem writes
　　the poet, not vice-versa.
The poet just cooperates.
Interrupted, the poem returns
　　beyond denial like a love
　　that's chosen, conjugal
　　and undeniable.

> Similarities
> are obvious even when
> they seem far-fetched.
>   Asked
> if he believed in God and why,
> one widower said, "I want
> to see my wife again."

While in the throes of writing a poem, Hazo feels bound by the poem until it's finished. Explaining the tremendous difficulty of bringing his poems to life, he says: "I often agonize over finding exactly the right word or phrase to convey the meaning or feeling I want to convey. I don't really control it—I am possessed by it; I become the servant of the poem until it is finished." Despite the exhausting nature of submitting to each poem, Hazo welcomes the process because, as a writer, that's where he lives and grows.

In the quotation above, Hazo is referring to being consumed by one poem—never two or three in different stages of production. "Every poem is jealous as hell," he quips. "You better not have another one circulating." Hazo insists that each poem occupies all of his time, all of his attention, until it's finished. "Eventually, the poem demands it. You start out with a flirtation, a line or a word, and after a while, the poem lets you know that it's time to get serious. We're in the galley together."

After more than sixty years writing poetry, Hazo insists that the emotional, mental, and physical commitment required by a poem is still as arduous as it was in the beginning. "Every poem has been a breach birth," he laughs. "There were no easy deliveries." Sometimes, he explains, a moment of pure luck ushers in a line or two almost perfectly—but that does not occur often:

I find writing the most exhausting kind of work. When I'm working on a poem or finished with a poem, I'm as dead tired as I can be— all the way through, I'm just beat … When you're writing a poem, your whole mind and everything about you is in the poem. It's in what you're doing, and when you're finished, it's as if somebody had taken a sponge and squeezed it dry. You fill up again and start absorbing things again, but at that moment you're out of everything. It's all there in the poem. You've given it away. (qtd. in Sokolowski, 237)

Despite the exhausting nature of the process, Hazo finds great satisfaction in getting a poem as close to "right" as he thinks it should be. That sometimes happens quickly, but it often comes through months—sometimes even years—of revision. The feelings of relief and fulfillment that invariably accompany the completion of a poem are usually short-lived; Hazo quickly begins to feel lonesome that the poem has ended and there's nothing to command his full attention: "I mean, there are things that are total, and writing a poem is one of them. I've never had a baby, but having a baby is one. Making love is one."

A Poem's Only Deadline Is Perfection

After you start to write it,
　　you belong to the poem.
　　　　　　　　　Your time
　　becomes the poem's time,
　　which ranges anywhere
　　from now to who knows when.
You're like a sculptor working
　　with mallet, wedge and file
　　to help the sculpture waiting
　　in a bulk of rock emerge.
Like something born in hiding,
　　a poem lets itself be found
　　the more you fret and work
　　to free it of its flaws.

Even when the poem seems complete,
   you're still not sure of a verb here,
   an adjective there.
                 You squander
   hours searching for alternatives
   until they both occur to you
   by chance while you're thinking
   of something else entirely.
There's no timetable.
               You pause
   when the poem makes you pause.
You write when the poem makes
   you write.
            Precedent means nothing.
Even when you think it's done,
   it's never done.
             You tell yourself
   you could have made it better,
   but the time for bettering is over.
Being a poet means
   you have to live with that.

Whether his poems end with a surprise turn of events, a philosophical musing, a new way of seeing the world, a devastating emotional revelation, or a metaphorical punch to the gut, the powerful last line is a significant hallmark of Hazo's poetry. "I work very hard on knowing when to end a poem—and how," he says. But he admits he didn't always know when to end a poem—and that some of his early poems continue after the poem is over. "Over the years," he says, "I learned that less is more." Hazo employs this strategy of restraint across all dimensions of his poetry: "My view of writing is that you shouldn't let it all hang out. It's best to hold back. Poetry by definition is an act of saying what can't be said. You hint at it. As Plato said, you speak by similitudes

… you try to reach a point where the language is so transparent that to the reader, it's hardly there" (qtd. in Sokolowski, 260).

Despite the flaws he now recognizes in some of his early work, Hazo asserts that he would never go back and revise his poems because he's a different man now than he was when he finished those poems—with potentially different views, attitudes, and ideas. By way of example, he speaks of Wordsworth, who revised his *Prelude* years after its original publication: "When he revised the middle section, he ruined it," Hazo says. "The version that he wrote when he was in his prime was his best poem. The revision was the poetry of a dried-out old man."

For Hazo, an important part of the writing process is having the faith to allow a poem to move in unplanned directions, perhaps even to become a completely different poem than the one he started writing: "I have poems that have been suggested by a single line, and when I finish, that line isn't even in the poem. It just did its job and then went off someplace else. It's very hard to let a certain line or idea go. Sometimes I've been determined to keep it in there—just because. Then I'll wake up one morning, read the poem, and realize that it doesn't belong in there at all."

The process of composing every poem ignites renewed learning for Hazo. "That's real learning," he explains. "You don't know what you know until you write it. You may think you do, but you don't. The poem gives it to you."

Another World

Whether it's ours or another's
a poem begins when it ends.
It has to be over to earn
entirety.
Re-reading
or re-hearing it, we learn
what it means in stages.

                              It may
take years.
                              There's always
more than we imagined.
        In the end we let the poem
have its way with us
        until we share the life
it summons, word by word.
                              The once of everything is twiced,
and we awaken to a world
        that's surer, braver, truer.

Ironically, Hazo says the poem "Making It Look Easy" was the most difficult poem to write, taking ages to complete and presenting many more challenges than he anticipated. A metaphor about "creativity in action," the poem is about a number of famous people who have perfected their crafts to such a high degree they literally make it look easy. Hazo explains, "Poetry or any art in its final expression often seems effortless. When poetic knowledge is actuated by the poet's creative intuition, the consummation, whether in drama, fiction, poetry, or, as mentioned in this poem, billiards, has this quality of effortless perfection. It's never a matter of mere technique." Although choosing which artists to highlight wasn't simple, the most troublesome part for Hazo was determining how to humanize the ideal of "perfection" by showing how it can operate in the hands of a regular person. After months of agonizingly unsatisfactory attempts, Hazo finally thought of his uncle, the pool master, and that was precisely the piece he needed.

Making It Look Easy

Whatever it is, Spencer Tracy
        had it—acting as if he wasn't
        acting, which is acting at its best.

So did Fred Astaire and Ginger Rogers
        swirling in "The Continental," Bojangles
        tapping, Michael Jackson
        at his peak, Nureyev leaping
        and Gene Kelly on his own.
Sampras in his prime made sport
        and grace synonymous.
                        Seferis
        in Beirut preserved within himself
        the Greece the Nazis never
        could defeat.
                        Greece lives forever
        and wherever in his poetry.
                                And that's
        the point.
                        There's one Seferis
        to a century, if that.
                                The same
        is true of those named
        heretofore who made a poem
        of their work.
                        Why bother with less
        when nothing better than the best
        should ever be imagined?
                                Let those
        who say that poetry is mere
        technique be damned.
                                They're thinking
        only of the tricks that inspiration
        nixes with impunity to let
        perfection happen...
                                I had
        an uncle who was tops in pool.

No one could match him.
                              Thirty
     years retired from the game,
     he took a pool shark's challenge
     as a dare.
                         Without a session
     to rehearse, he chalked his cue,
     then broke the rack and ran
     the table as of old.
                              The bet
     was made and paid, and that
     was that.
                         Even the loser
     was amazed to watch a master
     show him how poetically
     the art of 8-ball could be played.

Like Spencer Tracy, Fred Astaire, Pete Sampras, and the pool master, the real grace of Hazo's poetry is its seeming effortlessness. As Ryan Wilson asserts,

Hazo's artfulness is evident only to artists, while his poems themselves speak to the many. That is, he was "accessible" long before poets like Billy Collins and Ted Kooser, but he has never sacrificed artistic integrity for "accessibility." In a recent poem, Hazo asks "why / are we here except to share?" That rhetorical question might well be a kind of key to his aesthetics: without abandoning the rigors of technique, Hazo has always been aware that his poems must speak to the audience of the present, must "share" with an audience which has changed a great deal since he began writing and which continues to change. The poet must adapt to the audience of the moment, without forfeiting the good, the beautiful, and the true. Hazo has accomplished this astounding feat over six decades. (letter of support, US Poet Laureate nomination, 2019)

Although often possessed of a powerful political conscious-ness, Hazo's poetry never serves a particular political agenda. In-stead, it focuses exclusively on the human element of the political situation. He explains:

When literature is put to the service of a cause, it immediately ceases to be literature. It becomes propaganda. Maybe propaganda for a good cause, but propaganda nonetheless. . . . Good or bad, it usurps the cre-ative spirit that wants to support it. I'm for literature that has a political consciousness, since an awareness of people as political beings is vital. But I'm against partisan consciousness that destroys the creative spirit. (qtd. in Sokolowski, 274)

Regarding the politics of war, Hazo insists that no poet worth his salt has ever written a poem in praise of war. Having penned his share of poems about the devastation of war, Hazo focuses on individual human pain. After seeing a segment on television about the mother of a captain who was killed by snipers in Af-ghanistan, Hazo wrote "No Words for This." Based on her story about her son's last letter to her, Hazo's poem beautifully conveys the depth of this mother's love and anguish:

No Words for This

If a true poem is one
    you wish you never had
    to write, then this is it.
Don't read it just to say
    you've read it.
              That's like
    the traveler who went to Spain
    so he could say he went
    to Spain.

>   The words I've picked
>   have really picked themselves,
>   but what's not written here
>   is where the poem breathes . . .
>   The mother of a captain killed
>   by snipers read his final
>   letter postmarked on the date
>   he died.
>   She read it often
>   after that.
>   And every time
>   she closed the envelope, she slowly
>   licked it shut so that her tongue
>   could taste him in the last
>   thing he ever touched.

Using Wilfred Owen's World War I poems to exemplify the importance of the human element in war poetry, Hazo distinguishes between Owen's most famous poems—those he wrote from his experiences in the trenches—and those he wrote when he was wounded in the hospital, which Hazo believes more memorably convey the human drama. "Disabled," for example, tells the story of a soldier who has lost his legs. Having been sent home to a hospital in his hometown, he is completely at the mercy of his attendants. The last two lines of the poem are devastating, as the soldier is sitting in his wheelchair—just sitting there—thinking, "How cold and late it is! Why don't they come / And put him into bed? Why don't they come?"

No other vehicle delivers the human experience in quite the same way as an effectively penned poem—and that, Hazo insists, is why poetry makes a difference in our world: "The Greeks have a phrase: 'Only poetry can heal the wounds of death.' Religion and time won't do it. Only poetry can do it."

Poetic Technique

Hazo's early poems employ largely traditional metrics—iambic pentameter and various trimeter lines. Like many poets who are learning their craft through experimentation, Hazo initially felt comfortable imitating the techniques of previous patterns. After some time, however, he realized the metrics of Greek and Roman prosody were not made for the English language; they were adapted for the English language. He concluded that the normal length of expression for a human breath is three stressed syllables, regardless of how many unstressed syllables occur between them. (This aligned with Hopkins's theory of "sprung rhythm.") He therefore began to focus his attention on writing poems in which each line contained three stressed syllables along with various numbers of unstressed syllables, depending on the poem. The most significant stylistic evolution of his poetic technique over the years, this has become his signature metric because, as he asserts, it comes closest to the way he thinks and speaks.

Hazo has been in a class by himself throughout his writing career, always seeming to defy whatever was "fashionable" on the American poetry scene at the time. In a personal interview, author Mike Aquilina explained:

We had the confessional poets, who dominated after World War II and made a fetish of pathology. But Sam would have no part of that. He was just making beautiful poems. After the confessionals, we had the dominance of people like John Ashbery whose work is opaque. It's cultivated obscurity. Well, Sam has never gone by that aesthetic. Sam's work has a clarity, a simplicity—he owns his own voice, and he has just brought it to a pitching affection now. Sam is—as Longfellow was in the nineteenth century—rooted in his place. He's not a regionalist, but he's revered in Pittsburgh. We hear his voice, we recognize it as our own, and we love it because of its particular character. Sam has been his own man through all those fashions that have passed.

Although he moved away from traditional metrics more than forty years ago, Hazo still incorporates all of the "forms" in his poems—just differently. Aquilina continues, "Everything that he learned from forms, about the power of language—the power of the *sound* of language—is still in his work today. All of the forms are still present." He may not be writing iambic pentameter anymore, in other words, but important elements of his formal apprenticeship are evidenced in all of his work. As the editor of Hazo's recent collection (*When Not Yet Is Now*), James Matthew Wilson has developed insights about Hazo's idiosyncratic form, which actually "gives shape to the sound and rhythm of the language and allows him to say what he has to say." This, Wilson asserts, sets Hazo apart from many others:

Most contemporary poets who do not write in meter use "forms" that are ersatz, i.e., they do not really shape the rhythm of the language but merely the shape of the words on the page (typography); and, because their form is so superficial or irrelevant to poetic rhythm, they reshape their content to make it sound "poetic," by which is meant in this case, obscure, fragmentary, unintelligible, and inhuman. Like Hopkins, Sam has found a poetic form that makes it possible to hear his poems as poems while also allowing him to speak clearly and with significance on things that matter to actual human beings, as opposed to the editors of obscure poetry journals. (interview, January 18, 2019)

Hazo's poetic form, which has been influenced by formalism but reshaped and repurposed over the course of his career, can be claimed as his alone. Although he no longer ascribes to the complex technical demands of metrical prosody, elements such as balance, meter, and rhyme (internal, near, assonance, alliteration, consonance) still figure prominently in Hazo's poetry. And the one traditional form that Hazo truly enjoys and continues to produce is the ballad. He has penned a variety of compelling ballads complete with a formal ballad rhyme scheme (often ABCB) and common ballad characteristics such as simplicity of structure, style, and diction, dialogue, and repeated lines. His collection *Ballads and Duets* (2001) features eight of his favorites, but his success with the ballad structure extends beyond those chosen few. Although he won't commit to a favorite, "Ballad of the Jolly Broker" is, in his estimation, the most technically interesting and the most revealing of the poem's character. "Ballad of the Broken Tackle" has also stood the test of time in terms of both its technical composition and its message:

Ballad of the Broken Tackle

If you're squat as a rock, and you know how to block,
and the backs that you block for are shifty,
you can dream of a life with a Hollywood wife
and a ranch you'll own outright at fifty.

But the jackpots of fame and your love of the game
never match what you learn as a player.
You crouch in the dirt, and you play when you're hurt,
and you wake up one day, and you're grayer.

Though nobody sees when you're gone in the knees
so you flinch when you're running or bending,
you feel in your heart that you're coming apart,
and you know when you're nearing the ending.

Jim Otto would glow with a big double-O
on the jerseys he wore in his glory.
Today he needs care, and he's wheeled in a chair,
and that's just one man and his story.

Look hard at the rest of the worst and the best
and notice how much they're reliant
on braces and canes and some pills for their pains
that have left them subdued but defiant.

The owners ate well while you sweated like hell
to give the damn city a reason
to light up the sky like the Fourth of July
at the end of your winningest season.

Looking back you can see it's no bonus to be
number one in a league of achievers.
It just rouses the loud in the stadium crowd
and the rest of the paying believers.

Overlooking the noise, it's a game meant for boys.
At its best it's no more than a pastime.
But why were there tears despite all the cheers
when you limped off the field for the last time?

The last line of the ballad delivers the message poignantly. Although players may initially be motivated by the fame and enormous financial rewards of professional play, retirement often proves devastating for them. "You see their statement on TV—and sometimes they can't get through it without breaking down," Hazo says. "My theory is that it really had nothing to do with money or fame; it's just that when you have to leave something that you did at the level of the very best—you're leaving a lot of what is important in your life. You're essentially admitting that you just can't do it anymore. After being the best in baseball for eight years, Joe DiMaggio let a ball go over his head that he normally would have gotten. He came into the dugout, threw down his glove, and said 'That's my last game.' When asked why, he said 'I can't play and be Joe DiMaggio anymore.'"

Part of the reason people enjoy Hazo's public readings so much is because he precedes or follows each poem with either a philosophical musing about life, love, and human behavior or a wonderful human-interest story about friends, family, celebrities, and random people he has encountered throughout his life. He has been known to launch into recitations of poems by other poets and quotations by movie stars, world leaders, historical figures, Shakespeare, and the Bible—all without a single note in front of him! Audiences also continue to be astounded that Hazo has committed his own poems to memory, never so much as glancing at a book during the entire recitation. In short, Hazo's public readings are so much more than poetry readings. For an hour or more, Hazo delights, educates, thrills, entertains, and astounds his audiences, who depart knowing that poetry is alive and well and capable of speaking to our very souls.

Hazo admits that he enjoys reciting some poems more than others because they have proven to be crowd-pleasers. "A Toast for the Likes of Two" has been a consistent audience favorite, along with "Kak" and a few of his other family poems. And "In the Time of the Tumult of Nations" routinely receives spontaneous applause despite the generally accepted recitation protocol of reserving applause until the end of the program.

A Toast for the Likes of Two

Who was it wrote, "If women
    had mustaches, they would somehow
    make them beautiful.
                  Look
what they've done with breasts!"
Who disagrees?
                Doesn't the Bible
    say a woman just an inch
    from death will keep an eye
    for color?
            And don't philosophers
    assert that women sacrifice
    the ultimate on beauty's altar?
And love's . . .

Why scoff at that?
Are the male gods of money,
    fame, and power more deserving?
What's money but guilt?
                What's fame
    but knowing people you will never
    know will know your name?
What's power but pride translated
    into force?
                Are these worth more
    than what sustains us to the end?
Consider Bertha.
                Eighty, blind
    and diabetic, she believed that death's
    real name was Harold.
                        "I want
    to know what Harold has to offer,"
    she would say.
                    She'd seen
    her children's children's children
    and presumed she had a poet's right
    to give a name to death, if so
    she chose.
                Chuckling to herself,
    she rocked and waited for this last
    adventure in her life ...
                            Then
    there was Jane, who mothered seven
    and left unfinished all her art
    by choice as if to prove
    that incompleteness is the rule
    of life where nothing ends
    the way it should ... or when.

Two weeks before her funeral
she called all seven to her bed
to say, "I hope to see you all
again … but not right away …"
So here's to the honor of Bertha,
and here's to the glory of Jane!
Let them be spoken of wherever
beauty's lovers gather to applaud
the beauty of love.
                 Let them
not rest in peace but thrive
in everlasting action, doing
what they love the most.
                Who wants
a heaven that's equivalent to one
long sleep?
             Those crypted, supine
saints in their basilicas can keep
the dream of their Jerusalem.
                The soul
was meant for more than that.
Pray for us, St. Bertha.
Pray for us, St. Jane.

In his letter to the Library of Congress supporting Hazo's 2019 nomination for US Poet Laureate, scholar Ryan Wilson describes Hazo's steady and unrelenting commitment to his art:

[Hazo] has lived and written through wildly shifting aesthetic fashions, social upheavals, and political climates. And yet, Dr. Hazo has always had the courage to resist the perpetual temptation of the faddish. He has followed his vocation as a poet, not the vicissitudes of his times. Unlike many poets of his generation, Hazo has not destroyed himself, nor has he struck the tragic pose of those who idealize self-destruction, nor has he abandoned his beliefs for the sake of convenience or fame.

Rather, for more than sixty years, he has looked into the mirror of the silence, and he has brought back words that have cut through the noise and folly of his times, words that have shown his readers reflections of themselves as they are, not as they wish to be, words that have brought self-knowledge, and hope, and awe into the hearts and minds of his many readers.

Describing what writing poetry has meant to him throughout his lifetime, Hazo says:

Do you know what it means to do something where you are totally yourself? My aunt used to love to sew. When she sewed, the world could go to hell; she was completely herself sewing. I think every person has some pocket of attention that is just his or hers when he or she is doing it. Time means nothing. The only thing that matters is how well you're doing what you're doing, and that you can do it. If you ignore that, you're ignoring the most important thing in your life. That's what poetry is for me. No matter how agonizing it is when you're involved in the writing of a poem—however much you pay for the attention that it demands—you know that nobody else could be doing what you're doing except you. And that makes it all personal, and it makes it worth it.

Unlike Joe DiMaggio, Hazo can still be Sam Hazo. He remains true to himself without the need or desire for notoriety. Despite the passage of time, his writing continues to inspire and delight his readers with a spark of recognition as he articulates deeply held beliefs we are unable to express. Over more than sixty years of his writing career, we have come to rely on his always fresh perceptions of life and humanity. Through his inimitable voice, his poetry and prose contain the truths we crave—and they are particularly meaningful to us now "in the time of the tumult of nations." As presumptuous as it may sound, we can only ask for more.

The hard reality remains that Hazo's pen will one day run dry. When asked what he would like the world to remember most about his poetry, he replies with classic Hazo style: "That I didn't fake it."

Acknowledgments

Many thanks to my La Roche University colleagues who made my sabbatical possible: Lee Markowitz, the members of the Faculty Development Committee, Howard Ishiyama, and President Candace Introcaso. Without the uninterrupted time provided by the sabbatical, I may never have finished this book. Thanks also to my friends in the English Department: Michelle Maher, who chaired the department in my absence, and Josh Bellin, Linda Jordan, Ed Stankowski, and Sister Rita Yeasted, who provided constant encouragement and support. I am thankful for our two wonderful faculty assistants, Barb Bencsics and Stephanie Marks, whose kind and gracious help I'm sure I relied on far too much.

Adria Kelleher's skillful editing saved me when various obstacles stopped me in my tracks. She provided light and clarity where I most needed it, and there aren't enough foxgloves in the world to sufficiently thank her. Christine Abbott provided essential perceptual guidance early in the writing process—helping me to own my role as author and understand the book as my own. My student interns, Julia Felton and Mina Holland, conducted important research in the book's early stages, and Brian Bayer graciously agreed to read and comment on the completed draft when I was afraid to let anyone else see it. His honest and intelligent feedback guided my efforts during revision and gave me confidence to keep moving forward.

Thanks to Mike Aquilina, James Matthew Wilson, and Ryan Wilson for their insightful interviews. My discussions and email exchanges with them deepened my understanding of Hazo's work, and their scholarly contributions significantly enhance the story of Hazo's life. I appreciate the excellent staff at the Theodore M. Hesburgh Library archives for their patience when I almost certainly overstayed my welcome. And my sincere gratitude to Sarah Wear and the editorial board at Franciscan University Press for believing in my work, and to copy editor Ashleigh McKown for always knowing exactly what I meant to say.

My beautiful family—Rachel, Brian, and Sofy—you are my heart's joy and the most loving support team a mom could ever hope for. Jacqueline, David, Ian, Nicole, Alex, Mackenna, Jazzy Jim, and Marlene—your encouragement and faith in me are constant motivators. Bill—your quiet patience while I wrote the book and calm assurances that I could do it each time I convinced myself otherwise fueled me to the finish line; thank you for being my *Solution Man*.

And finally, my eternal thanks to Sam Hazo, who so generously shared his journals, photographs, personal International Poetry Forum archive, stories, memories, philosophies, feelings, professional contacts—and, most of all, his precious time—while I researched and wrote this book over a period of four years. Working with him has been a sincere joy and an extraordinary honor, and I hope this book sufficiently reflects my deep admiration and respect.

Bibliography

Chabon, Michael, and Ayelet Waldman. *Kingdom of Olives and Ash: Writers Confront the Occupation.* HarperCollins, 2017.

Furlong, Thomas Francis. "Samuel Hazo: The Challenges of a Double-Edged Awareness." MA thesis, Pennsylvania State University, 1983.

Hazo, Samuel, dir. *Actors and Actresses Reciting Poems.* International Poetry Forum, 2010.

Hazo, Samuel. *And the Time Is: Poems, 1958–2013.* Syracuse University Press, 2014.

———. *Ballads and Duets.* Byblos, 2001.

———. *Discovery and Other Poems.* Sheed and Ward, 1958.

———. *If Nobody Calls, I'm Not Home: The Open Letters of Bim Nakely.* Wiseblood Books, 2020.

———. *Once for the Last Bandit: New and Previous Poems.* University of Pittsburgh Press, 1972.

———. *Outspokenly Yours, Commentaries: 1993–2016.* Word Association Press, 2017.

———, dir. *Poets Reciting Their Own Poetry.* International Poetry Forum, 2010.

———. *Silence Spoken Here.* Marlboro Press, 1988.

———. *Thank a Bored Angel: Selected Poems.* New Directions, 1983.

———. *The Autobiographers of Everybody: A Mosaic Portrait of the International Poetry Forum.* International Poetry Forum, 2011.

———. *The Feast of Icarus: Lyrical Essays.* Stuart-Wright, 1984

———. *The Feast of Icarus: Memoir and Myth.* Lambing Press, 2017.

———. *The Holy Surprise of Right Now.* University of Arkansas Press, 1996.

———. *The Next Time We Saw Paris*. Wiseblood Books, 2020.

———. *The Pittsburgh That Stays Within You*. 5th ed. Word Association, 2017.

———. "The Poet and Society: Freedom to Create." *Humanitas* 1, no. 3 (Winter 1966): 263–71.

———. *The Power of Less: Essays on Poetry and Public Speech*. Franciscan University Press, 2019.

———. *The Wanton Summer Air*. North Point Press, 1982.

———. *The World within the Word: Maritain and the Poet*. Franciscan University Press, 2018.

———. *They Rule the World*. Syracuse University Press, 2016.

———. *To Paris*. New Directions, 1981.

———. "When Clocks Have No Hands." *Pittsburgh Quarterly* (Spring 2019).

———. *When Not Yet Is Now*. Franciscan University Press, 2019.

International Poetry Forum Digital Archive, 1966–2009. Grace Library Collection, Carlow University. https://www.carlow.edu/International_Poetry_Forum_Archives.aspx.

Judt, Tony. *Ill Fares the Land*. Penguin, 2011.

"Poetic Justice." *Pitt Magazine* (2004): 6.

"Poetic Moments: Samuel Hazo Presents Asides from the International Poetry Forum." *Pittsburgh Post-Gazette*, February 15, 2015.

"Poetry Forum Utters Its Final Verse." *Pittsburgh Post-Gazette*, February 13, 2009.

Reich, Robert. *The Common Good*. Vintage, 2019.

Sokolowski, David Paul. "The Poetry of Resistance." PhD thesis, Marquette University, 1991.

Wilson, Ryan. Letter to Robert Casper nominating Samuel Hazo for US Poet Laureate, February 17, 2019.

Wood, David. *What Have We Done: The Moral Injury of Our Longest Wars*. Little, Brown, 2016.

Index of Poems